Decorative paint

Techniques & Ideas

John Wiley & Sons, Inc.

This book is printed on acid-free paper. ∞

Copyright © 2009 by Meredith Corporation, Des Moines, Iowa. All rights reserved

Published by John Wiley & Sons, Inc., Hoboken, New Jersey
Published simultaneously in Canada

No part of this publication may be reproduced, stored in a retrieval system, or transmitted in any form or by any means, electronic, mechanical, photocopying, recording, scanning, or otherwise, except as permitted under Section 107 or 108 of the 1976 United States Copyright Act, without either the prior written permission of the Publisher, or authorization through payment of the appropriate per-copy fee to the Copyright Clearance Center, 222 Rosewood Drive, Danvers, MA 01923, (978) 750-8400, fax (978) 646-8600, or on the web at www.copyright.com. Requests to the Publisher for permission should be addressed to the Permissions Department, John Wiley & Sons, Inc., 111 River Street, Hoboken, NJ 07030, (201) 748-6011, fax (201) 748-6008, or online at http://www.wiley.com/go/permissions.

Limit of Liability/Disclaimer of Warranty: While the publisher and the author have used their best efforts in preparing this book, they make no representations or warranties with respect to the accuracy or completeness of the contents of this book and specifically disclaim any implied warranties of merchantability or fitness for a particular purpose. No warranty may be created or extended by sales representatives or written sales materials. The advice and strategies contained herein may not be suitable for your situation. You should consult with a professional where appropriate. Neither the publisher nor the author shall be liable for any loss of profit or any other commercial damages, including but not limited to special, incidental, consequential, or other damages.

For general information about our other products and services, please contact our Customer Care Department within the United States at (800) 762-2974, outside the United States at (317) 572-3993 or fax (317) 572-4002.

Wiley also publishes its books in a variety of electronic formats. Some content that appears in print may not be available in electronic books. For more information about Wiley products, visit our web site at www.wiley.com.

ISBN: 978-0-696-23844-4

Printed in the United States of America
Second Edition
10 9 8 7 6

Introduction

If you're looking to add depth and interest to your walls, it's as easy as applying a new coat of paint. Painting is a fast and inexpensive way to change the style and ambience of a room. Solid-color walls are fine, but when you enhance them with a decorative painting technique, you add an extra layer of sophistication and creativity to your room. Whether you want to infuse your walls with subtle tone variations using washes and blends of color, create the illusion of fabric panels, or make a bold statement with stripes and blocks of coordinating hues, the basic painting information and specific techniques on the following pages will guide you to success. Designed for painters of all skill levels, this book will get you started on the path to discovering your unique creative style.

The book is divided into three sections. The first section outlines the principles of color selection, illustrates the tools you will need for basic painting, takes you through the process of preparing your walls and applying that first all-important base coat, and gives you an overview of decorative painting fundamentals. The second section presents detailed, step-by-step instructions and photographs of 51 stunning paint finishes. Many favorites, such as faux-fabric finishes, bold stripes and blocks, and glaze techniques, are included. Decorative paint treatments such as aging and metallic finishes are perfect for today's popular old-world and contemporary decorating styles. Updated versions of traditional favorites such as marble, Venetian plaster, and murals make these sometimes challenging techniques easier to execute. The third section illustrates decorative paint finish combinations and outside-the-box ideas to inspire you and fuel your creativity. An idea gallery and selection of patterns helps further inspire and guide you. Armed with this book, you can transform your walls from boring to beautiful.

Contents

IN THIS SECTION

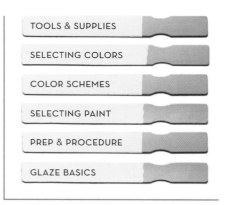

Paint Basics

Decorative painting can be a rewarding and creative experience, but a good foundation of planning and preparation is necessary to ensure the success of any project you undertake. This section is devoted to the information you need to plan your painting project with confidence.

Choosing a color scheme is one of the first steps in planning any new decorating project. A basic understanding of color starts with the color wheel. The color wheel is a universal visual tool that organizes colors and shows the relationships between them. The next step is building a specific color scheme. Collecting inspirational material such as photos from books and magazines, fabric patterns, and paint manufacturers' brochures is a good way to build your idea file and narrow your color preferences. With a color scheme decided, you are ready to make your paint purchase. This section lists the characteristics of paint types and sheens and includes tips on calculating paint coverage so you can approach the paint aisle at your local retailer with confidence.

This section also gives you an overview of the tools used for basic painting and measuring as well as specific tools used for decorative paint effects. It includes a description of each tool, its use, and a photo so you can locate it at your home center or paint store. A primer of basic painting information takes you through the process of preparing walls for painting and applying the first base coat of paint. A discussion of glazing—from mixing instructions to creating effects—answers common questions and takes the guesswork out of this decorative painting fundamental.

Once you have the essential information you need to plan and start your painting project, you are ready to select a decorative paint finish.

Tools & Supplies

Good-quality tools are one of the more important elements for any successful painting endeavor. Well worth the initial investment, they can make the job go smoothly and efficiently. Properly cared for quality tools will last a long time. The following tools are used for basic painting. Specialized decorative painting tools are described on page 17.

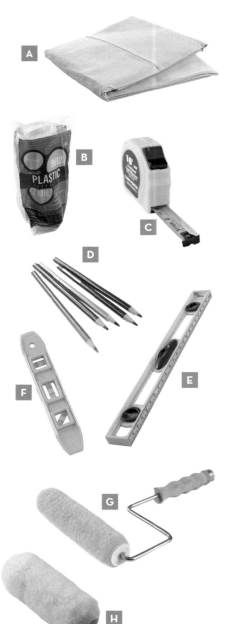

A. CANVAS DROP CLOTH
Rubber-back canvas drop cloths absorb liquid on the top while preventing it from leaking through to the backside. In addition they are heavy enough to stay put whether used on the floor or over furnishings. Be sure to choose one with a tight weave for best protection.

B. PLASTIC DROP CLOTHS
Plastic drop cloths are an inexpensive and popular choice with many painters; however they can be slippery on the floor and may shift easily when placed over furniture. In addition plastic does not absorb liquid so it becomes easy to transfer spills to unwanted areas. Drop cloths are also used for some decorative painting techniques.

C. TAPE MEASURE
For measuring a room's basic dimensions or marking large increments for stripes, blocks, and panels, a tape measure is an indispensable tool. Tape measures are available in several lengths. Unless your rooms are very large, a 25-foot size is best because it is long enough to measure most room dimensions but small enough to be lightweight.

D. COLOR PENCILS
Color pencils are a better choice than graphite pencils for any marking job because the markings do not smudge and will blend with the paint, whereas graphite pencil marks will smudge. Drawing pencils come in sets that contain a variety of colors and they are available at art and craft supply retailers. Use a pencil that is closest to the paint color you are using.

E. LONG LEVEL
Use a long carpenter's level to accurately mark long vertical and horizontal lines. Levels may be purchased in a variety of lengths. A 2-foot length is best for most jobs, but if you are marking very long lines you may want to consider a 3-foot size or longer. If you purchase a level with printed measurements, you can measure and mark at the same time.

F. TORPEDO LEVEL
Though not as essential as a long level, a bullet level comes in handy when working in tight areas or marking short lines. It is lightweight, easy to maneuver, and every bit as accurate as a long level.

G. STANDARD ROLLER FRAME
Standard roller frames are available in a variety of styles. Choose one that feels balanced and fits your hand well. Roller frames that have a threaded hole in the end of the handle are designed for adding an extension that allows you to paint ceilings and high areas.

H. STANDARD ROLLER COVER
Roller covers that slip over a roller frame vary in material and nap length. Short-nap synthetic fiber or foam rollers are generally used for smooth surfaces. Medium- and thick-nap synthetic fiber rollers are best for covering rough or textured surfaces. Standard roller covers are 9 inches wide.

I. MINI ROLLER FRAME WITH COVER

Mini rollers are used to apply paint in small areas and where a standard-size roller is too large. They are available in a variety of widths from 2 to 6 inches. Roller cover choices include short- and long-nap synthetic fiber and foam.

J. BRUSHES

Angled trim brushes are used for cutting in along ceilings and woodwork as well as for painting trim. The tapered and angled bristles create a crisp, clean line ideal for detail work. Use a wide brush for overall coverage. Read the label and select a brush that is compatible with the type of paint you intend to use and the surface you're painting.

K. PAINT TRAY

A paint tray has a deep reservoir that holds paint and is deep enough for dipping the roller. When you pull the roller across the ramp, the ribbed surface distributes the paint evenly and sends the excess back to the reservoir.

L. PAINT TRAY LINER

For easy cleanup use a disposable plastic paint tray liner. When you've finished painting, let the leftover paint dry in the liner before throwing it away. If you have a metal paint tray that has become rusty, use a tray liner to avoid paint contamination.

M. PLASTIC CONTAINER WITH MEASUREMENTS

Plastic containers with printed measurements and lids have several uses. They hold small amounts of paint when you are base-coating trim or tight spots. With their preprinted measurements they also make measuring and mixing glazes easy. The lids, often purchased separately, seal the containers for short-term storage. They're available in quart and gallon sizes.

N. 5-GALLON BUCKET

A 5-gallon bucket is handy for big jobs. Use it for mixing large quantities of glaze or tinting texture compounds. It is essential for cleaning during room preparation and cleanup after completing the project. Between jobs it can be used for storing hand tools and supplies.

O. 5-IN-1 TOOL

A multipurpose tool is essential for basic painting projects. The blunt section of the leading edge of this tool is used for opening cans. The pointed section of the leading edge is good for scraping narrow areas or opening cracks for patching. The front edge can be used for scraping or applying surfacing compound. And the curved area removes excess paint when cleaning rollers.

P. PUTTY KNIFE

Putty knives, available in a variety of widths, are used to apply surfacing compound when repairing surface imperfections on walls prior to painting. They are also used to apply texture compounds for a variety of decorative painting techniques.

Q. STIR STICK

Wooden stir sticks are handy for mixing paints and glazes prior to painting. They are available at no charge if you ask for them when you purchase paint.

R. LINT-FREE COTTON CLOTHS

Use lint-free cloths to remove dirt and dust, clean up spills, and wipe away mistakes. White, 100-percent-cotton cloths are the best choice. Avoid using colored fabric that may deposit unwanted dye stains on surfaces. Choose cloth that is free of particles that will rub off on walls and leave a fuzzy residue. Cotton cloths are also used for manipulating paint-and-glaze mixtures in many decorative paint techniques.

S. PAINTER'S TAPE

Specialty painter's tape is used to mask off areas before painting. There are two grades of adhesive backing for painter's tape. Medium-adhesion tape is often used on woodwork that has a nonporous finish, such as gloss or semigloss paint. It adheres and seals well and will stay put for the duration of the painting project. If left on too long, however, it may pull off the finish when removed. Low-tack painter's tape for delicate surfaces is used to temporarily mask off stripes, borders, and wall panels. It is often removed immediately after painting an area. Because of its mild adhesive quality it will not pull off base-coat paint when removed. Both types of painter's tape are available in a variety of widths.

Selecting Colors

Choosing color for home decor projects can be overwhelming. To make the process less intimidating, start with a basic understanding of color theory and the color wheel.

The Color Wheel

The color wheel, a universal tool used by designers and artists, organizes the visible spectrum of colors and shows the relationships among them. It consists of 12 colors laid out in three categories in a circular format. It is easy to use and indispensable when visualizing color combinations that work together to build a color scheme.

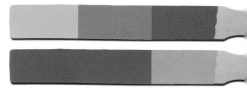

PRIMARY COLORS

Equally spaced on the color wheel, the first group of colors—red, yellow, and blue—are called primary because they cannot be derived by mixing other colors. In fact they are the colors that must be mixed to create all others.

SECONDARY COLORS

The next group of colors is referred to as secondary. Orange, violet, and green are derived from mixing equal parts of two primary colors; for example, red plus yellow make orange. Each secondary color lies between the two primary colors that combine to create that color.

TERTIARY COLORS

The last color group, called tertiary colors, is derived from mixing equal parts of a primary color with its adjacent secondary color; for example, blue and violet create blue-violet. There are a total of six tertiary colors and they are located between the primary and secondary colors that, when combined, create that color.

Color Schemes

There are five basic color schemes or methods of grouping colors to create pleasing, no-fail combinations.

MONOCHROMATIC

This scheme utilizes various shades and tints of a single color. Shades are derived by adding black to a pure hue while tints are derived by adding white. Monochromatic schemes create a sense of serenity, elegance, and unity in a space. Using a wide range of tints and shades within the scheme creates interest and variety.

TRIADIC

Triadic color schemes utilize three colors that are equidistant on the color wheel. These are visually exciting schemes because they create interest through contrast. Using tints and shades of pure hues moderates the effect.

ANALOGOUS

Analogous colors are located side by side on the color wheel. Similar to monochromatic color schemes, this combination is soft, creating a soothing, low-intensity atmosphere. The addition of a second adjacent color creates another layer of interest.

COMPLEMENTARY

Using two colors positioned directly opposite on the color wheel creates a complementary color scheme. Whether interpreted in pastel tints or vibrant pure hues, this color scheme is almost always lively and dynamic.

ANALOGOUS/COMPLEMENTARY

Adding complementary accents to an analogous color scheme imparts a pop of interest to the harmonious pairing of side-by-side hues. Using pure hues creates a strong impact while using tints and shades yields a softer effect.

Building a Color Scheme

To help you with the task of selecting a pleasing decorating palette, look through books and magazines to build a collection of images with color schemes that inspire you. Study patterned items with color schemes that capture your interest, such as fabric swatches or wallpaper samples, and use the color wheel to identify those schemes. Take note of how the colors are in balance. Which one is dominant and what are the accent colors? Visit a paint center and pick up inspirational brochures, color scheme cards, and paint chips that illustrate the color schemes you are considering.

Once you've chosen your working color scheme, decide on proportions. This balancing act is key to getting the desired results. Choosing a dominant color, the one you'll use on the wall, is the first step. Most paint companies have computer visualization programs either onsite or online that you can use to try your color ideas in virtual reality. Some of the programs allow you to use your own digital room photo as a background for color testing. Other programs contain a gallery of room backgrounds for you to choose from.

Once you've narrowed your choices, it is a good idea to purchase a few paint samples and base-coat a 4-foot-square area directly on your wall. This will enable you to observe how changes in natural and artificial light throughout the day and evening will affect the colors you're considering.

Selecting Paint

Once you have made your final color selection, you must make a number of additional decisions before finalizing your paint purchase.

Oil or Latex

Latex water-base paints are the most commonly used paints for interior finishes. They are environmentally friendly, fast-drying, easy to work with, and simple to clean up. The technique instructions in this book list latex paints almost exclusively.

Oil-base paints offer advantages in some situations that might outweigh those provided by latex paints. They offer better coverage than water-base paints and can cling to a wider range of surfaces. Oil-base paints have a slower drying time than latex, making them a better choice for some time-intensive decorative painting techniques. On the downside oil-base paints and their solvents are not as environmentally friendly as latex paints, and cleanup is more difficult.

A New Generation of Latex

In recent years with environmental concerns taking center stage in the world community, it has become increasingly important to develop green products of every description, and paint is no exception. Paint manufacturers have responded to consumer demand for environmentally friendly water-base formulations. With the changing chemical compositions in paint products, questions arise as to how the new generation of paint formulas will perform when executing decorative painting techniques.

In order to answer those questions, the editors of this book researched and developed a testing program for the latest paint formulations. A series of 13 tests was performed using the participating paint brands. The tests included low VOC (volatile organic compound), no VOC, and mold- and mildew-resistant formulas. There proved to be almost no difference in the overall performance of any paint formulation tested.

The chemical formulations all worked equally well, although paint thickness became an issue with painted-stripe techniques. Thin paint may adhere less well than thick paint, resulting in part of the top coat coming

Thin-bodied paint failed to adhere well, so paint peeled off when the tape was removed.

off when tape is removed. To be safe always paint a sample board with the paint you plan to use to make sure it will perform properly.

Decorative Paint Test Results

Heavy-body paint works best for taped-off horizontal stripes.

Avoid paint lift off when stamping by using low-sheen paint.

For best coverage use a low-sheen base coat when stenciling.

Adding glaze medium to paint changes the sheen to semigloss.

All paint formulations work well with sponging techniques.

Use the same sheen when sponging two colors together.

For combing use heavy-body paint to create crisp-edge stripes.

Strié techniques work best with semigloss sheen paint.

Fabric looks need more pressure when brushing through heavy paint.

Crosshatch techniques work well with any paint formulation.

Plastic wrap techniques are successful with any formulation or sheen.

Ragging techniques work great with any paint formula or sheen.

Paint Sheen

Latex paint is available in a variety of sheens. The five standard paint sheens are flat, eggshell, satin, semigloss, and gloss. Each sheen designation refers to how much light the paint reflects or the shininess of the finish. Some paint manufacturers consider satin and eggshell to be the same sheen. Others categorize eggshell after flat and add a bit more shine and durability to the formulation. When choosing paint always check out sheen samples before making a decision. The following is a description of each paint sheen, its primary characteristics, and its uses:

FLAT

Flat paint is the least reflective of all sheens. It absorbs light and therefore hides many surface imperfections. Since it hides blemishes so well, you can often apply only a single coat. However it has the lowest durability of all paint formulations and fails to stand up well to scrubbing. It is most commonly used on walls and ceilings of living rooms, bedrooms, dining rooms, and hallways. It is not recommended for kitchens and baths.

SATIN/EGGSHELL

A step more reflective than flat paint, satin sheen offers a silky finish and is more stain-resistant and easier to clean than flat paint. It is often used on walls where regular cleanup is required, such as children's rooms, kitchens, and baths. It is an ideal sheen to use for many decorative painting and faux-finishing techniques.

SEMIGLOSS

Walls in kitchens and baths benefit most from this sheen because they receive regular scrubbing. Its reflective quality accentuates architectural details on woodwork and cabinetry but also reveals imperfections on any surface. Semigloss is often used for decorative painting and faux-finishing techniques because, when mixed with glaze medium, it imparts depth and visual dimension to any finish.

GLOSS

This sheen has the highest reflective qualities. It is most often used on cabinets and woodwork. It is the most durable of all the sheens and handles regular washing best. Since it highlights imperfections more than any other sheen, it is seldom used on walls.

TIP

How Much Paint?

A good guideline for estimating paint for your project is to allow 1 gallon per 300 square feet of wall surface. To calculate square footage of the walls, multiply the length of each wall by the height and add all of the figures. (You don't need to deduct the square footage of doors and windows unless you have oversize windows or numerous windows or doors on a wall.) Divide by 300 to get the number of gallons needed for **one coat**. Aim to have a little paint left over for touch-ups.

Prep & Procedure

Organization and preparation are the key ingredients for success in any painting project. The up-front effort is well worth the time spent because it will make the job go smoothly and produce professional-looking results. Follow the tips, techniques, and procedures below to help ensure a successful, low-stress painting experience.

Ready the Room

Clearing the space is the first step in preparing a room for painting. After shutting off power to the room, move out everything you can; that includes light fixtures, ceiling fans, window treatments, heat registers, and switchplates. Shield the exposed outlets with painter's tape. If you must leave anything in the room, move it to the center and cover it with plastic sheeting. (Old sheets or newspapers are insufficient; paint can soak through them.)

Protect the floor with disposable drop cloths, and tape them down so you won't slip. To improve ventilation open windows and turn on fans if necessary.

Repair Imperfections

For smooth painting surfaces that will ensure a quality finish, repair imperfections in the walls. There are fillers available appropriate for each type of wall surface. Inquire at your local paint or home center to find the right filler for your walls. When using filler products be sure to follow the manufacturer's instructions. Follow the procedures outlined below for different types of repairs. Once repairs are complete sand all surfaces smooth. Wipe away or vacuum up all dust.

SMALL HOLE
Press surfacing compound into the hole with a putty knife. Build up the compound in thin layers until the surface is even and then sand smooth.

LARGE HOLE OR DENT UP TO 4 INCHES
Cover the damaged area with fiberglass mesh tape before applying a fast-drying plaster compound on top. After the compound has dried, sand the area; repeat if needed. Seal the patched area with primer to promote a consistent finish.

POPPED NAILHEAD
Drive a screw into the wall about 2 inches below the nail to secure the drywall to the framing, slightly recessing the screw. Hammer the popped nail in, leaving a slight dent in the wall. Patch the nail and screw area with lightweight surfacing compound.

CRACK
Use rubberized filling compound to repair a crack. If the crack is less than ¼ inch wide, you'll need to widen it with a utility knife. Fill the crack, cover the wet compound with fiberglass mesh tape, and then apply more compound. Let dry then apply more compound. Let dry overnight before adding more layers of compound if needed; sand smooth and seal with primer.

GAPS BEHIND TRIM
Fill spaces between woodwork and the wall using a latex caulk and caulking gun. Remove the excess with a damp sponge and let dry overnight.

MOLDING
Fill imperfections with wood filler; let dry. Sand and seal the entire molding after patching.

Clean All Surfaces

To guarantee good adhesion when applying a new coat of paint, thorough cleaning is essential. Wear vinyl gloves to protect your hands from chemicals. Wash the walls with a mild ammonia-base or alkaline household cleaner. For grease stains use trisodium phosphate detergent (commonly known as TSP). Use hydrogen peroxide solution for mold or mildew stains. Rinse all surfaces and let dry.

Prime Before Painting

Applying primer is a good idea if your walls have never been painted because it prevents excessive paint absorption. On older walls apply a stain-blocking primer to keep marks from showing through. If you're painting over dark colors or strong patterns, several coats of primer may be necessary.

Painting Procedure

TRIM

Begin by applying all desired coats of finish on moldings before starting on the ceilings and walls. Once the trim is dry, cover it with painter's tape, working over one small area at a time, without stretching the tape, and pressing firmly. Use the edge of a credit card or the back of your fingernail to seal edges well.

CEILING

Paint the ceiling next. Pour ½ inch of paint into a bucket or paint tray. Dampen a tapered trim brush with water and blot onto a paper towel before dipping the lower third of the brush bristles into the paint. Tap each side of the loaded brush against the bucket rim. Paint a 3-inch-wide strip to outline the ceiling. This is referred to as "cutting in." Next dampen a paint roller with water and then wrap it in a lint-free cloth and blot dry. Insert an extension into the roller handle. Then load the roller by dipping it into the deep area of the paint tray and rolling it on the tray ramp until covered evenly. Slowly roll the paint onto the ceiling, working across the width rather than the length. Let the paint dry and apply another coat if necessary.

WALLS

Paint the walls last. Working on one wall at a time, first cut in at the ceiling line, in the corners, and along the trim. Use a paint roller to roll out the large surfaces, being sure to blend the cut-in bands while they're still wet. Holding the roller handle with both hands, slowly roll paint onto the wall—first up, then down, then up, applying the paint in a W shape. Reload the roller often. Work in 2-foot-wide sections, always keeping a wet edge of paint. For areas where a paint roller won't fit, use a wide paintbrush. Apply the paint in long strokes, brushing up to unload the brush, then down to set the paint, then up to remove brush marks. Work up from the bottom of the wall in fairly narrow sections. Be careful around the taped-off moldings; if you brush toward the tape, you may push paint underneath or build it up along the edge. After the first coat is dry, apply a second coat if needed. Clean up spills and mistakes right away; wet paint is much easier to remove. If you take a short break, wrap wet brushes and rollers in plastic rather than washing them. As soon as the final coat of paint has set, remove the tape by pulling it off at a 90-degree angle. Avoid going so fast that the tape tears or so slowly that adhesive remains on the surface.

TIP

It's best to apply two thin coats rather than one heavy coat. A heavy coat can dry unevenly and leave visible areas where the paint overlaps.

Color variations will be most obvious at midwall, so don't switch to a new paint can there; instead, use different cans on opposite walls or change cans at a corner.

When you open a can of paint, place the lid in plastic to prevent drips and drying. Punch holes inside the can rim to let paint drain back into the can. Stir the paint then pour a quantity into a bucket or tray. To prevent contamination do not use paint directly from the can.

To help reduce hand fatigue when cutting in paint, hold the paintbrush as you would a pencil. A tapered brush works best for this procedure. Begin by stroking the loaded brush along the taped-off edge for a short distance, then brush outward to fade the edges.

When rolling on paint, use up-and-down strokes to apply the paint in a W shape across a 2-foot-wide section. Continue rolling up and down, working horizontally across the section to fill in unpainted areas.

To prevent paint buildup on the recessed rim of the can, use a hammer and nail to punch holes through the rim. This allows excess paint to drain back into the can, preventing drips and ensuring a tight seal when the lid is replaced.

Cleanup

When you have finished your painting project, clean and store paintbrushes and rollers. To clean brushes and rollers, scrape off as much paint as you can, then brush or roll them over newspaper. For latex paint rinse the brushes and rollers under running water until the water is clear then wash them with mild soap and water. Hang brushes to dry. Stand rollers up to dry. If you use oil-base paint, you'll need solvent. Leave brushes and rollers in the solvent until it clouds, then replace it. Continue doing this until the tools are clean, then wash them with mild soap and water. To protect them from damage, replace rollers and brushes in the original plastic sleeves before storing.

Glaze Basics

Glaze is one of the more important fundamentals of decorative painting. With the exceptions of stencil, stamp, and solid-coverage techniques such as stripes and blocks, most decorative painting techniques involve a glaze element. The glaze is generally applied over a base coat of solid color and then manipulated using a variety of tools and methods to create pattern and visual texture. Some techniques require only one glaze coat while others require multiple layers.

Mixing

To create a colored glaze, mix glaze medium with paint to yield a translucent mixture that, when applied over a base coat of paint, allows that solid layer of color to show through from underneath. The effect imparts visual depth. Glaze medium is simply paint without pigment. The basic glaze formula includes all of the necessary ingredients that make up paint minus pigment. It has a milky appearance but dries clear. When paint is added the mixture becomes a translucent version of the color that's been mixed with it.

When mixing glaze a standard guideline is to mix one part paint to four parts glaze. While testing your chosen technique on sample boards, you may find that this formula is too heavily pigmented or too thinly pigmented for the effect you want to achieve. For testing mix small quantities and then adjust the paint-to-glaze medium ratio as needed. The addition of small amounts of paint conditioner will aid with workability and slow the drying process, allowing you more time to work the technique.

Technique

The amount of glaze needed for a decorative paint effect depends on the application technique. When the effect requires overall glaze application followed by removal of small amounts of glaze, the coverage is roughly the same as that of a solid coat of paint. For consistent color on nearly solid coverage techniques such as faux-fabric effects, it is important to mix enough glaze to complete the job. When small amounts of glaze are applied and then blended out to a thin layer, the coverage is much less. For effects that rely on color variations to add depth and interest, smaller batches may be mixed as needed because slight inconsistencies in color add to the effect. Use plastic containers with printed measurements to assure consistent mixes.

As the samples below show, glaze may be applied in varying amounts to create different results. Building up one or more thin layers of color yields a subtle effect. One thick layer gives a heavier final appearance.

Applying one very light coat of glaze changes the base coat only slightly while adding subtle nuances of color.

Adding another layer of glaze deepens the effect and adds another layer of visual depth.

A thick layer of glaze nearly covers the base coat entirely and changes the wall color dramatically. In this case the base coat of color creates subtle highlights.

Specialty Tools

Many decorative techniques may be achieved using simple household items or standard painting tools. The specialty tools and brushes designed for specific techniques, described below, are available at crafts retailers and home centers.

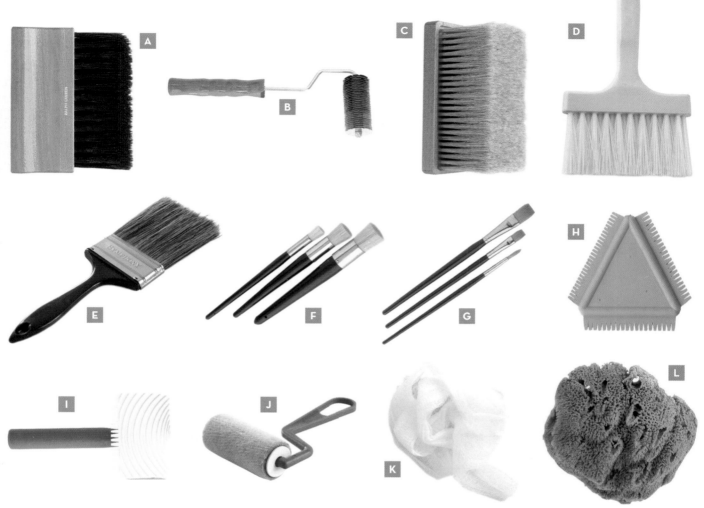

A. WEAVER BRUSH
A weaver brush is used to create the look of linen or denim.

B. CHECK ROLLER
A check roller is used to create the look of faded threads on a denim fabric technique. After a weaver brush establishes the basic warp and weft pattern, a check roller is rolled across the wall both vertically and horizontally to scratch through the glaze and reveal fine lines of base-coat color.

C. STIPPLING BRUSH
Use a stippling brush with a pouncing motion to create dense stippled texture or to blend glaze colors together.

D. WALLPAPER PASTE BRUSH
A Used for strie techniques, wallpaper brushes are available in a variety of widths.

E. STRIÉ BRUSH
A strié brush is used to drag through a coat of glaze from ceiling to floor and create fine streaks that resemble silk fabric.

F. STENCIL BRUSHES
Stencil brushes are available in a variety of sizes. Use large ones for overall coverage and smaller ones to fill in details.

G. ARTIST'S BRUSHES
Flat and round artist's brushes in a variety of sizes are used for handpainted motifs and details.

H. TRIANGLE COMB
Combing tools create fine pinstripes when run through a top coat of glaze. Smaller combs may be purchased and large ones may be homemade from a squeegee.

I. WOODGRAINING TOOL
A woodgraining tool, pulled through wet glaze using a drag-and-rock motion, creates the look of knotty wood planks.

J. STENCIL ROLLER
Using a stencil roller for stenciling large wallpaper stencils makes the job fast and the coverage consistent. Look for these specialty rollers at crafts or paint retailers.

K. CHEESECLOTH
Cheesecloth is used for a variety of decorative paint techniques. Used dry it removes glaze, leaving a mottled pattern. Used damp it softly blends and smudges glaze, creating subtle tone variations.

L. SPONGE
The size and pattern of the holes in a sponge determine the textural effect it creates.

Decorative Paint Techniques

Once you have determined your color scheme and arrived at a basic wall color, you are ready to choose a decorative painting technique. The technique you choose depends on the role you want your walls to play in the overall room design. Subtle color variations or fine-pattern textures add an overall feeling of warmth and intimacy. Bold effects should be reserved for focal-point walls where you wish to highlight architectural features or create a backdrop for a furniture grouping.

This section features step-by-step instructions for 51 decorative finishes from basic techniques, such as stripes, faux fabrics, and layered glazes, to more creative techniques, such as aging and freehand painting. Each project is labeled with a skill level designation of beginner, intermediate, or advanced. Even if a technique seems to be above your level of experience, give it a try and practice on a sample board until you are comfortable with the process. Then you will be able to approach a blank wall with confidence.

Each technique includes a list of tools and supplies needed to complete the project. Paint sample swatches help you visualize the color palette used in the paint treatment. Helpful tips are included throughout to further your understanding of a process or to suggest alternative design ideas. Some of the projects include technique variation color samples and real-room photographs of optional colors and designs.

Linen

Throughout the centuries civilizations have valued linen for the practicality of its open, breathable weave and the beauty of its natural texture and striated nubby fibers. The linen technique is often executed in the natural tones of cream to light tan, but a myriad of beautiful pastel hues may be used to enhance a more varied color scheme.

The linen look can be achieved with standard off-the-shelf paint and glaze products. However the technique can be further enhanced by using a specialty glaze that contains fibers in the formulation, producing a texture that simulates the realistic, nubby feel of linen fabric. A solid base coat is applied first and allowed to dry, then the linen glaze is rolled on. While the glaze is wet, a specialty brush, called a linen weaver brush, creates the crosshatch pattern that resembles woven fabric.

Fresh and sophisticated this classic effect works in elegant, traditional, and casual rooms. Its subtle texture is a feast for the eyes and wraps a room in natural warmth.

SKILL LEVEL

Intermediate

SPECIAL TOOLS

a. Level with printed ruler

b. 2-inch-wide low-tack Painter's tape

c. Glaze medium

d. 7-inch linen weaver brush

a.

b.

c.

d.

TOOLS

Dark tan colored pencil

Tape measure

Drop cloth

Stir sticks

Paint tray

Standard roller frame with 9-inch roller cover

2-inch tapered trim brush

Plastic container with printed measurements

Large plastic bucket

Lint-free cotton cloths

PAINT

Semigloss or satin latex for both colors

LIGHT PARCHMENT FOR BASE COAT

DARK WHEAT FOR GLAZE COAT

Faux Fabrics

Linen

INSTRUCTIONS

Mask ceiling, baseboards, and trim with painter's tape. Paint the entire wall in the light parchment base-coat color. Paint two coats if necessary. Leave tape on; let the paint dry overnight.

The linen technique is executed in a series of vertical panels. The panels should be narrow enough in width so that you can work comfortably and quickly; a width between 24 and 36 inches is generally manageable. To divide the room into panels of equal width, first measure the total width of each wall in inches. Next divide the total wall width by the desired panel width to determine the number of panels. You can end panels in corners or wrap them around corners, but because maneuvering the weaver brush around a corner can be tricky, ending panels in corners is easiest.

Use a plastic container with printed measurements to measure 4 parts glaze to 1 part dark wheat paint into a clean bucket. Mix enough glaze for the entire project so that the intensity of the glaze color is consistent from panel to panel. The total amount of glaze mixture should equal the amount of base-coat color applied for one-coat coverage (see page 13).

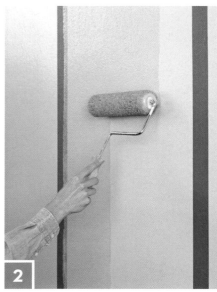

To lay out the panels, use a tape measure and colored pencil to measure and mark all the walls with an upper and lower mark for each panel interval. Then use a long level to draw vertical lines from ceiling to baseboard, connecting upper and lower marks at each panel interval. The level will ensure that the lines stay vertical and parallel to one another.

Because every other strip is painted the first day and the remaining strips are painted the next day, tape off alternating sections with the low-tack painter's tape. After trimming with the glaze mixture along the ceiling and baseboard of the first taped-off panel using a trim brush, use a well-saturated roller to apply glaze to the remainder of the panel. Quickly roll long, vertical strokes from ceiling to floor across the entire width of the panel to even out the glaze.

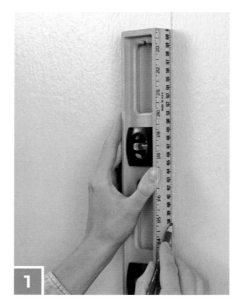

To create the horizontal weave lines, begin at the top left-hand corner of the panel and drag the linen weaver brush across the panel from left to right, applying firm enough pressure to bend the bristles.

Immediately drag the brush back over the first stroke in the opposite direction using the opposite side of the bristles.

Wipe the brush with a damp cloth after each horizontal pass to remove excess glaze buildup. Continue brushing the horizontal weave pattern from left to right all the way down the wall.

For the vertical weave start at the ceiling in the upper left-hand corner of the panel and, using light pressure so the brush skims the wall without erasing the horizontal lines, brush straight down to the bottom of the panel in one continuous stroke. If you must use a ladder to reach the ceiling, make a few dry runs to practice stepping down the ladder as you pull the brush through the glaze.

Remove the vertical strips of painter's tape immediately after dragging and while the glaze is still wet. Complete the first series of panels and let them dry overnight before taping and painting the final series, repeating Steps 2–6. To abut the seams place the tape on top of the dried glaze along the edge where the sections meet.

TIP

The specially formulated linen glaze can be tinted with any shade and brand of semigloss paint, or you can choose from a variety of premixed tinted linen glazes.

When working on a panel that is located in a corner, drag the horizontal strokes in one direction only, from the corner outward.

Variation

The linen effect can work beautifully in any color but is most effective when rendered in pastel hues. Trying the technique on small decorative accessories such as linen storage boxes or drawer-front panels on furniture is an excellent way to practice your skills before tackling an entire room.

Dry-Brush Linen

SKILL LEVEL
Beginner

SPECIAL TOOLS
a. Glaze medium

b. Wallpaper brush

c. Lint-free cotton cloths

a.

b.

c.

TOOLS
2-inch-wide low-tack painter's tape

Drop cloth

Paint tray

Standard roller frame with 9-inch roller cover

Stir sticks

Plastic container with printed measurements

PAINT
Eggshell latex for both colors

BRIGHT GREEN FOR BASE COAT

WHITE FOR TOP COAT

If you're looking to introduce visual texture on plain-color walls without actually creating a raised surface, this technique works beautifully. The easy-to-paint treatment yields high impact with a minimum of work and requires only one brush—a wallpaper brush. Simply dip the brush into a paint-and-glaze mixture, then stroke it horizontally and vertically across the wall to produce the touchable texture of soft, nubby linen. Whether you enhance the existing hue on your walls or start with a fresh base coat of paint, with very little prep you can brighten your walls with the open-weave look of homespun linen fabric in only a couple of hours.

The casual look of this technique lends itself well to cottage, country, vintage, and transitional decorating styles. Brush on a small amount of color for a soft, understated look to enhance a frilly pastel color scheme. Or build the color intensity to make a bold statement for a backdrop of rustic, primitive, or mod furnishings. Let your personal style be your guide to create a look as unique as you are.

INSTRUCTIONS

Mask ceiling, baseboards, and trim with painter's tape. Paint the entire wall in the green base-coat color. Paint two coats if necessary. Leave tape on; let the paint dry overnight.

Use a plastic container with printed measurements to measure and mix 2 parts glaze to 1 part white paint. After testing on an area, adjust the glaze mixture if necessary. For more information about glazing, refer to Glaze Basics on page 16.

Pour the glaze mixture into a clean paint tray and lightly dip the tips of the wallpaper brush into the glaze mixture. Drag the brush across the nubs on the slanted area of the paint tray to evenly distribute the glaze into the brush and remove excess glaze.

Lightly brush across a clean lint-free cloth to remove more paint and dry the brush.

Using a very light pressure and short strokes, drag the brush across the wall horizontally on a 48-inch-square section of the wall. Reloading the brush as necessary and, following Steps 2–3, continue to dry-brush paint on that section until the desired depth of color is achieved.

Brush vertical strokes over the horizontal strokes to create a crosshatch linenlike-weave effect. Allow to dry.

Repeat brushing horizontal and vertical strokes as necessary to gradually build visual texture and depth of color as desired. Periodically stand back from your wall to judge your work. If some areas become too dense or intense with color, dry-brush over them with the green base-coat color.

Denim

Nothing says casual living like a softly faded denim shirt or a comfortable pair of worn denim jeans. Give your walls that same relaxed look by painting on a faux-denim wall finish that's perfect for any casual living space. There are many cool blue paint hues from which you can choose to create a denim finish that will blend with today's most popular color schemes. Simply pick a light and dark value of your favorite hue and you'll be ready to dress your walls in casual style.

With a little planning for the room's layout and two specially designed tools—a denim weaver brush and a check roller, the denim technique is easy to accomplish. The weaver brush simulates the weft and warp of denim fabric when pulled horizontally and vertically through a rolled-on coat of wet glaze. The check roller is made up of notched metal discs. When rolled over a section of weaver-brushed wet glaze it creates fine lines that imitate the look of faded fabric threads. The special tools required for this technique represent a moderate investment but denim painting projects can go beyond walls. Try this technique on desks, dressers, headboards, or small storage chests to create unique furniture with a laid-back look.

SKILL LEVEL

Intermediate

SPECIAL TOOLS

a. Level with printed ruler

b. Painter's tape

c. Glaze medium

d. Denim weaver brush

e. Denim check roller

a.

b.

c.

d.

e.

TOOLS

Tape measure

Blue color pencil

Drop cloth

Stir sticks

Paint tray

Standard roller frame with 9-inch roller cover

2-inch tapered trim brush

Plastic container with printed measurements

Large plastic bucket

Lint-free cotton cloths

PAINT

Semigloss finish for both colors

PALE BLUE FOR BASE COAT

DARK BLUE FOR GLAZE COAT

TIP

If the thread pattern created by the check roller seems to disappear, wait about one minute then roll over the area again after the glaze has had time to set enough to hold the added texture.

When working on a panel that is located in a corner, drag the horizontal strokes in one direction only, from the corner outward.

Denim

INSTRUCTIONS

Mask ceiling, baseboards, and trim with painter's tape. Paint the entire wall in the pale blue base coat color. Paint two coats if necessary. Leave tape on; let the paint dry overnight.

The denim technique is executed in a series of vertical panels. The panels should be narrow enough that you can work comfortably and quickly; a width between 24 and 36 inches is generally manageable. To divide the room into panels of equal width, first measure the total width of each wall in inches. Next divide the total wall width by the desired panel width to determine the number of panels. You can end panels in corners or wrap them around corners, but because maneuvering the weaver brush around a corner can be tricky, ending panels in corners is easiest.

Using a plastic container with printed measurements, measure 4 parts glaze to 1 part dark blue paint into a clean bucket. Mix enough glaze for the entire project so the intensity of the glaze color is consistent from panel to panel. The total amount of glaze mixture should equal the amount of base-coat color applied for one-coat coverage (see page 13).

1

To lay out the panels, use a tape measure and colored pencil to measure and mark all the walls with an upper and lower mark for each panel interval. Then use a long level to draw in vertical lines from ceiling to baseboard, connecting upper and lower marks at each panel interval. The level will ensure that the lines stay vertical and parallel to one another.

2

Because every other strip is painted the first day and the remaining strips are painted the next day, tape off alternating sections with low-tack painter's tape.

3

Using a trim brush trim with the glaze mixture along the ceiling and baseboard of the first taped-off panel. Then use a well-saturated roller to apply glaze to the remainder of the panel. Quickly roll long vertical strokes from ceiling to floor across the entire width of the panel to even out the glaze.

4

To create the horizontal weave lines, begin at the top left-hand corner of the panel and drag the denim weaver brush across the panel from left to right, applying firm enough pressure to bend the bristles. Immediately drag the brush back over the first stroke in the opposite direction by using the opposite side of the bristles.

5 Wipe the brush with a damp cloth after each back-and-forth pass to remove excess glaze buildup. Repeat the process making a total of four strokes over the same area. Continue brushing the horizontal weave pattern all the way down the wall.

6 To make the vertical weave lines, start at the ceiling in the upper left-hand corner of the panel and, using light pressure so the brush skims the wall without erasing the horizontal lines, brush straight down to the bottom of the panel in one continuous stroke. If you must use a ladder to reach the ceiling, make a few dry runs to practice stepping down the ladder as you pull the brush through the glaze.

7 To make the thread lines, run the check roller in horizontal passes over the entire brushed panel. Apply firm pressure to remove enough glaze to create a random pattern of lines. To remove excess glaze buildup, frequently roll the check roller firmly across a damp cloth.

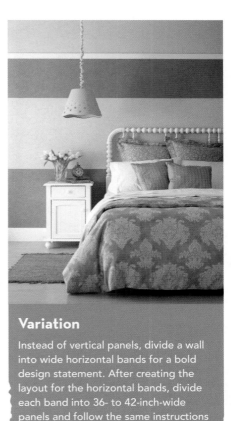

8 Run the check roller vertically through the panel. Make additional short horizontal and vertical passes to create additional detail. Complete the entire panel. Immediately remove the tape while the glaze is still wet.

9 Complete the first series of panels and let them dry overnight before taping and painting the final series, repeating Steps 3–9. To abut the seams place the tape on top of the dried glaze along the edge where the sections meet.

Variation

Instead of vertical panels, divide a wall into wide horizontal bands for a bold design statement. After creating the layout for the horizontal bands, divide each band into 36- to 42-inch-wide panels and follow the same instructions to execute the technique.

Suede

Whether in fashion or home decor, the soft tones and supple feel of brushed suede enchant the senses and make a truly upscale statement as almost nothing else does. You can give your walls the look and hand of authentic suede when you use a specially formulated suede paint. Applied with a brush or specialty roller right out of the can, suede paint dries to a low nap and has a hand-brushed appearance. Here the effect is enhanced by brush-blending two colors together to create even more visual contrast. Alternately applying the paint colors using a large brush and employing a crisscross blending technique is the secret to creating an enhanced color variation that catches the light and surrounds the room in visual warmth.

The faux-suede wall treatment is a perfect choice to lend an air of sophistication to rooms furnished in casual styles whether they are traditional, transitional, or modern.

SKILL LEVEL

Beginner

SPECIAL TOOLS

a. 4-inch-wide paintbrush

a.

TOOLS

2-inch-wide low-tack painter's tape

Drop cloth

Paint tray

Standard roller frame with 9-inch roller cover

PAINT

Eggshell latex for base coat, suede-finish latex for top coats

LIGHT GREEN FOR BASE COAT

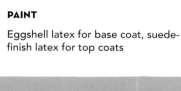

MOSS GREEN SUEDE FOR TOP COAT

DARK GREEN SUEDE FOR TOP COAT

INSTRUCTIONS

Mask ceiling, baseboards, and trim with painter's tape. Paint the entire wall in the light green base-coat color. Paint two coats if necessary. Leave tape on; let dry overnight.

1

Dip the 4-inch-wide paintbrush into moss green suede paint and, using large X strokes, begin to block in an irregular-shape section of wall approximately 28 inches square.

2

Without cleaning the brush, dip into the dark green suede paint and, using large X strokes, blend with the moss green suede paint. The amount of dark green you apply is optional. This wall shows approximately 70 percent moss green and 30 percent dark green.

3

After lightly blending the two colors of green suede paint in the first area, continue by blocking in an adjacent area with the moss green suede paint using X strokes.

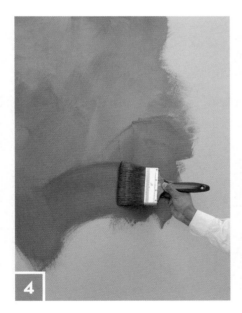

4

Add dark green suede paint to the second area and continue to blend.

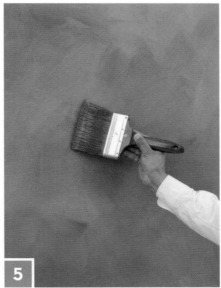

5

After filling in a large area, but before the paint has completely dried, go back over the area, adding moss green and dark green suede paint and blending until the desired result is achieved.

6

For a smooth, low-contrast look, blend the paint colors thoroughly. For a high-contrast look, only lightly blend the colors together. Remove tape; allow to dry.

SKILL LEVEL

Intermediate

SPECIAL TOOLS

a. Level with printed ruler

b. Plastic drop cloths

c. Glaze medium

d. Painter's tape

e. Natural sponge

a.

b.

c.

d.

e.

TOOLS

Graph paper

Tape measure

Drop cloth

Stir sticks

Paint tray

Standard roller frame with 9-inch roller cover

2-inch tapered trim brush

Colored pencil

Plastic container with printed measurements

Large plastic bucket

Lint-free cotton cloths

PAINT

Semigloss latex for all colors

PALE ORANGE FOR BASE COAT

TERRA-COTTA FOR GLAZE COAT

DARK BROWN FOR ACCENT GLAZE COAT

Leather

Leather, a staple in home decor, is beautiful and durable and gains character and patina over time. You can create the luxurious timeworn look of leather on your walls. Pressing plastic onto the wall over a rolled-on coat of wet glaze is the key to creating the pattern and texture. To further suggest the look of a custom-upholstered surface, the technique is rendered in rectangular panels. Because the plastic is applied differently on each panel, the result is varied and realistic. Working in manageable taped-off sections, one person can do the technique alone; work with a partner and the process is even easier. Earthy tones of brown and tan are the best color choices for a natural appearance, but the color ranges of hand-dyed leather can be inspiration for a more colorful rendition. Walls that are uninterrupted by windows and doorways are best for this technique so the full impact of the upholstered panels can be viewed and appreciated. No matter what your taste is, rugged or elegant, the classic look of leather is at home in living spaces that call for lived-in style.

Leather

INSTRUCTIONS

Mask ceiling, baseboards, and trim with painter's tape. Paint the entire wall in the light orange base-coat color. Paint two coats if necessary. Leave tape on; let the paint dry overnight. Remove ceiling tape.

Execute the leather technique in a series of rectangular panels. The panels should be narrow enough in height and width so you can work comfortably and quickly; a measurement between 36 and 42 inches is generally manageable. To divide the room into panels, first measure the total height and width of each wall in inches. Draw a sketch on graph paper to help you visualize how the panels should be arranged on the wall. The panels do not all have to be exactly the same size. You may make adjustments as needed. You can end panels in corners or wrap them around corners, but because maneuvering the plastic around a corner can be tricky, ending panels in corners is easiest.

Using a plastic container with printed measurements, measure 4 parts glaze to 1 part terra-cotta paint into a clean bucket. Mix enough glaze for the entire project so the intensity of the glaze color is consistent from panel to panel. The total amount of glaze mixture should equal the amount of base-coat color applied for one-coat coverage (see page 13).

For each panel use scissors to cut a piece of plastic drop cloth about 24 inches longer and wider than the rectangle; set aside.

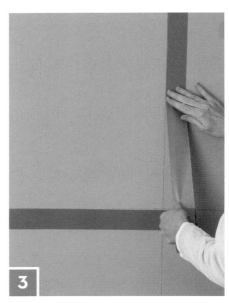

To begin laying out the panels, use a tape measure and colored pencil to measure and mark all the walls with an upper and lower mark for each vertical line. Then use a long level to draw in the lines to connect the upper and lower marks at each panel interval. The level will ensure that the lines stay vertical and parallel to one another.

Use a tape measure and colored pencil to measure and mark all walls for horizontal lines. Then use the level and pencil to draw in the lines to complete each rectangular panel.

Because alternating panels are painted first and allowed to dry before painting adjacent panels, tape off alternating panels with low-tack painter's tape.

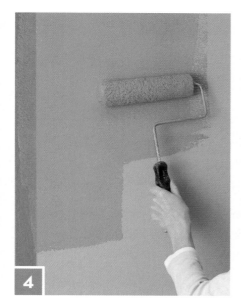

4

Using a trim brush trim with the glaze mixture along the ceiling or baseboard of the first taped-off panel. Then use a well-saturated roller to apply glaze to the panel. Quickly roll long vertical strokes across the entire width of the panel to even out the glaze.

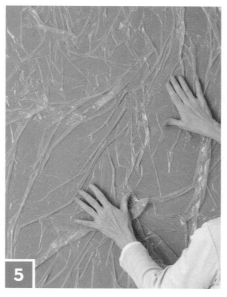

5

While the glaze is wet, apply a piece of precut plastic to the panel. Arrange the plastic as desired, letting it form random wrinkles. Press it flat with the palms of your hands. Avoid dragging your fingers across the plastic because lines will appear.

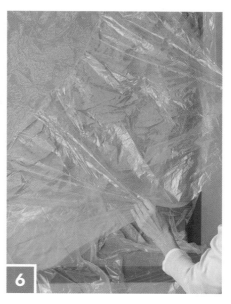

6

Starting at the top left-hand corner, peel the plastic off. Avoid dragging the plastic through the wet glaze or it will smear the pattern. Remove the tape immediately after removing the plastic. If glaze has seeped under the tape, immediately remove it with a wet cloth. Allow to dry. Repeat the process for every taped-off panel. Remove all tape and allow to dry.

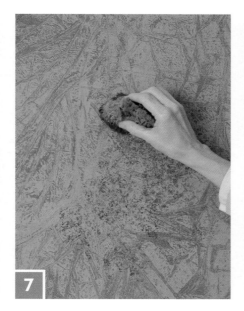

7

After all panels have been glazed and dried, retape alternating panels as in Step 3. In a plastic container, mix 4 parts glaze to 1 part dark brown paint. Dampen a natural sponge and pick up a small amount of the dark brown glaze, then lightly apply on each panel to create an irregular dappled pattern. Allow to dry.

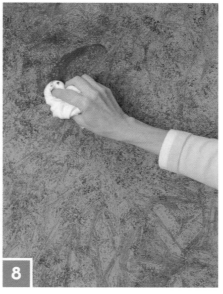

8

Use a damp lint-free cloth to wipe a sheer coat of glaze over the entire section. This enhances the terra-cotta color by creating an aged effect. Remove the tape and let dry. Repeat the process for each panel.

TIP

The leather technique works on any smooth surface. Tabletops, drawer fronts, chests, and cornices are merely a few items that can become real style standouts with a faux-leather treatment.

To further enhance an upholstered look, add upholstery tack borders to wall panel seam lines or furniture surfaces.

Study upholstery samples, handbags, shoes, and other leather items for inspiration as you plan your leather color scheme.

SKILL LEVEL

Intermediate

SPECIAL TOOLS

a. Level with
   printed ruler

b. 2-inch-wide
   low-tack
   painter's tape

c. Pearlescent
   glaze medium

d. Strié brush

a.

b.

c.

d.

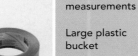

TOOLS

Drop cloth

Stir sticks

Paint tray

Standard roller
frame with 9-inch
roller cover

2-inch tapered
trim brush

Tape measure

Brown color
pencil

Plastic container
with printed
measurements

Large plastic
bucket

Lint-free
cotton cloths

PAINT

Semigloss latex for both colors

OFF-WHITE FOR BASE COAT

GOLD FOR GLAZE COAT

Silk Strié

The shimmering reflective quality of silk fabric imparts elegance and sophistication to a home's decor. And the opulent look of silk wall coverings may be achieved with ease at a fraction of the cost of silk.

Pearlescent glaze and a special strié brush are the secrets to this elegant faux-fabric technique. The pearlescent quality of the glaze produces a softly shimmering patina. The strie brush has long, soft bristles that create very fine, soft, and slightly uneven streaks when pulled through the glaze top coat to simulate the look of raw silk. If you wish to avoid investing in a strie brush, you can create a similar look with an inexpensive wallpaper brush, but the streaks will be more pronounced.

This elegant finish adds upscale luxury to formal living and dining rooms or to private spaces such as bedrooms or baths. During the day sunlight playing off the walls will radiate a warm glow, and soft lamplight or candlelight will enhance the effect in the evening hours.

Silk Strié

INSTRUCTIONS

Mask ceiling, baseboards, and trim with painter's tape. Paint the entire wall in the off-white base coat color. Paint two coats if necessary. Leave tape on; let the paint dry overnight.

The silk strié technique is executed in a series of vertical panels. The panels should be narrow enough in width so you can work comfortably and quickly; a width between 24 and 36 inches is generally manageable. To divide the room into panels of equal width, first measure the total width of each wall in inches. Next divide the total wall width by the desired panel width to determine the number of panels. You can end panels in corners or wrap them around corners, but because maneuvering the strié brush around a corner can be tricky, ending panels in corners is easiest.

Using a plastic container with printed measurements, measure 4 parts pearlescent glaze to 1 part gold paint into a clean bucket. Mix enough glaze for the entire project so the intensity of the glaze color is consistent from panel to panel. The total amount of glaze mixture should equal the amount of base-coat color applied for one-coat coverage (see page 13).

1

To lay out the panels, use a tape measure and colored pencil to measure and mark all the walls with an upper and lower mark for each panel. Then use a long level to draw in vertical lines from ceiling to baseboard, connecting upper and lower marks at each panel. The level will ensure that the lines stay vertical and parallel to one another.

2

Since every other strip is painted the first day and the remaining strips are painted the next day, tape off alternating sections with low-tack painter's tape.

3

Use a trim brush to trim with the glaze mixture along the ceiling and baseboard of the first taped-off panel. Then use a well-saturated roller to apply glaze to the remainder of the panel. Quickly roll long vertical strokes from ceiling to baseboard across the entire width of the panel to even out the glaze.

4

Draw the strié brush through the glaze from top to bottom in one continuous motion, creating a vertical pattern in the wet glaze. If you must use a ladder to reach the ceiling, make a few dry runs to practice stepping down the ladder as you pull the brush through the glaze. Wipe the excess glaze off the brush with a lint-free cloth and repeat until the panel is complete.

5

Remove the vertical strips of painter's tape immediately after dragging and while the glaze is still wet. Complete the first series of panels and let them dry overnight before taping and painting the final series, repeating Steps 2–4. To abut the seams place the tape on top of the dried glaze along the edge where the sections meet.

TIP

When choosing paint colors use a neutral hue or one in the same color family as the top glaze coat for best results.

To reduce the amount of metallic shimmer in the final finish, add clear glaze medium to the glaze mixture.

Variation A

You can take the strié technique from shimmering elegance to casual fun by using standard glaze medium instead of metallic pearl medium. This creates a nonreflective finish that serves as a stylish backdrop for decor accents that are funky and functional.

Variation B

Instead of using a light-color base coat, try using a hue that's a bit darker topped with a vibrant-hued glaze to lend pizzazz to a hip color scheme.

Rag Rolling

Rag rolling has been used for decades to create interesting visual texture on walls. The method creates a pattern by using a rolled-up rag to remove colored glaze or paint that has been applied to a base-coated wall. The process can be time-consuming and demanding, requiring you to keep a constant supply of rinsed, damp rags on hand. To render the job easy, fast, and failproof, create a homemade rag-rolling tool. Interfacing fabric from a sewing center, a standard paint roller cover, and a few rubber bands are all that's required to make a tool that takes the tedious work out of the process. This finish works with every decorating style and is especially effective for camouflaging flaws and imperfections on old plaster walls.

SKILL LEVEL

Beginner

SPECIAL TOOLS

a. Two standard 9-inch roller frames with covers

b. Glaze medium

a.

b.

TOOLS

2-inch-wide low-tack painter's tape

Drop cloth

Stir sticks

Paint tray

2-inch tapered trim brush

Plastic container with printed measurements

Large plastic bucket for mixing glaze

Rubber bands

15-inch square of interfacing (not fusible web)

Lint-free cotton cloths

PAINT

Semigloss latex for both colors

PALE ORANGE FOR BASE COAT

GOLDEN ORANGE FOR GLAZE

INSTRUCTIONS

Mask ceiling, baseboards, and trim with painter's tape. Paint the entire wall in the pale orange base-coat color. Paint two coats if necessary. Leave tape on; let the paint dry overnight.

Using a plastic container with printed measurements, measure 5 parts glaze to 1 part golden orange paint into a clean bucket. Mix enough glaze for the entire project so the intensity of the glaze color is consistent. The total amount of glaze mixture should equal the amount of base-coat color applied for one-coat coverage (see page 13).

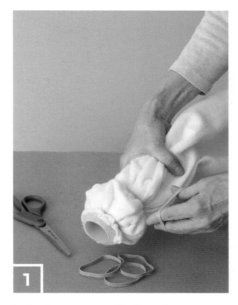

1 Make the ragging tool by loosely wrapping and bunching the interfacing around the 9-inch paint roller cover. Gather the interfacing as you go and secure with rubber bands. Dampen and wring out the homemade ragging roller cover and install it on the roller frame.

2 Starting at the top of the wall, cut in and roll glaze onto the wall in an irregularly shaped 4-square-foot area, using the remaining 9-inch roller.

3 Immediately roll through the glaze with the homemade ragging roller. Roll in different directions to remove glaze and create a mottled appearance.

4 Working quickly roll glaze onto an adjacent area, slightly rolling into the edge of the previously rag-rolled section.

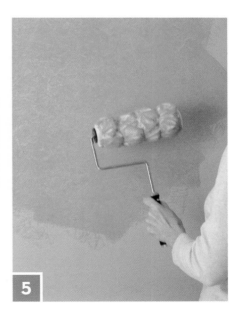

5 Use the rag roller to remove glaze, creating a mottled pattern. When the rag roller becomes saturated with glaze, remove the excess with a damp cloth. Do not immerse the roller in water to rinse it or it will retain too much moisture. A wet roller would dilute the glaze mixture when you apply it to the wall and remove too much glaze.

Graduated Color

Three green hues casually blended with a mini paint roller create the softly undulating visual effect in the living room below. Reminiscent of a misty landscape, the paint finish requires work to achieve a subtle effect, so it is a good idea to paint a sample board until you feel comfortable with the process. A special painting medium, available at paint retailers and home centers, is the key to success. Known as paint conditioner, it slows the paint drying time when added to interior latex paint colors, making blending easy.

SKILL LEVEL

Intermediate

SPECIAL TOOLS

a. 3 mini roller trays

b. Paint conditioner

c. 3 mini rollers

a.

b.

c.

TOOLS

2-inch-wide low-tack painter's tape

Drop cloth

Stir sticks

Standard-size paint tray

Standard roller frame with 9-inch roller cover

2-inch tapered trim brush

3 plastic containers with printed measurements

PAINT

Satin-finish latex for all colors

DARK MOSS GREEN FOR BASE COAT

MEDIUM MOSS GREEN FOR BLENDING

LIGHT MOSS GREEN FOR BLENDING

INSTRUCTIONS

Mask ceiling, baseboards, and trim with painter's tape. Paint the entire wall in the dark moss green base-coat color. Paint two coats if necessary. Leave tape on; let the paint dry overnight.

Pour one color of green paint into each plastic container. Add 3 tablespoons of paint conditioner to 2 cups of paint in each container and mix thoroughly. Prep three small roller trays by pouring one shade of green paint into each. Roll one small 4-inch roller into each color.

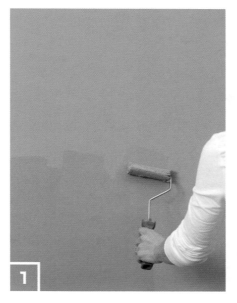

1

Roll the darkest green paint color onto the bottom third of the wall, moving the roller up and down as you work horizontally, making a jagged edge. Roll the medium green color in the same way onto the middle third of the wall.

2

Roll the lightest green color onto the top third of wall. There should be a loose, jagged line where each color meets another.

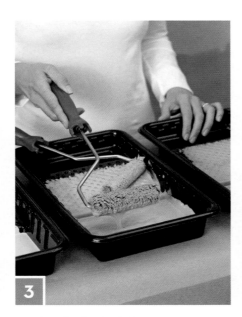

3

Dip the roller for the darkest green paint into the medium green paint. This will make the blending process between the dark and medium green sections much easier.

4

Roll the medium green paint onto the wall, blending the colors together at the point where the dark green and medium green meet. As you blend roll up and down in a slightly diagonal pattern, turning the roller and making jagged shapes as you move horizontally across the wall. Repeat this process until you're satisfied with the results, dipping into the medium green paint as needed.

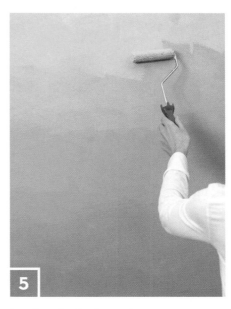

5

Dip the roller for the medium green paint into the light green paint. Blend the medium green and light green paint colors where they meet, following the procedure in Step 4. Let dry.

Brush & Pounce Blend

Subtle is the word that best describes the soft-hue brush & pounce blending technique. This blended finish is easy to execute with the aid of a homemade pouncing tool used to blend two colors of wet paint and create clouds of color. The simple tool consists of a dampened large natural sponge wrapped inside a piece of faux-lamb's wool fabric purchased from a fabric store. Practice the method first on a piece of scrap wallboard or cardboard to experiment with color and choose the amount of blending you desire. Two people working together speed the process. One person crosshatches the paint colors onto the wall, and the other uses the homemade pounce to complete the blending.

SKILL LEVEL

Beginner

SPECIAL TOOLS

a. Natural sponge

b. 6-inch-wide paintbrush

a.

b.

TOOLS

2-inch-wide low-tack painter's tape

Drop cloth

Stir sticks

Paint tray

Standard roller frame with 9-inch roller cover

2-inch tapered trim brush

Faux-lamb's wool fabric

Rubber band

PAINT

Semigloss latex for both colors

LIGHT BLUE FOR BASE COAT

DARK BLUE FOR TOP COAT

INSTRUCTIONS

Mask ceiling, baseboards, and trim with painter's tape. Paint the entire wall in the light blue base-coat color. Paint two coats if necessary. Leave tape on; let the paint dry overnight.

1

Dampen the natural sponge and wring out all excess moisture. Wrap it in faux-lamb's wool fabric and secure with a rubber band. Trim away excess fabric.

Brush on the base coat color using the 6-inch-wide paintbrush. Fill in an irregularly shaped area approximately 2 feet square.

2

While the base-coat area is still wet, pick up a small amount of dark blue paint on one corner of the brush and dab onto the wet light blue paint in a few places.

3

While the paint is wet, begin to blend the colors using the pouncing tool. Gently tap the pouncing tool onto the wall to create a softly mottled appearance. Avoid dragging the pouncing tool.

4

Move to an adjacent area and repeat Steps 2 and 3.

5

Continue to pounce-blend until the desired effect is achieved. After you have finished the wall, stand back and evaluate the result. If there are areas that need more work, wait until the paint has dried thoroughly and then rework as needed.

SKILL LEVEL

Beginner

SPECIAL TOOLS

a. 2 plastic
   containers
   with printed
   measurements

b. Paint
   conditioner

c. 2-inch tapered
   trim brush

a.

b.

c.

TOOLS

2-inch-wide
low-tack
painter's tape

Drop cloth

Stir sticks

Paint tray

Standard roller
frame with 9-inch
roller cover

PAINT

Semigloss latex for both colors

GOLDEN YELLOW FOR BASE COAT

BRIGHT PINK FOR GLAZE COAT

Brush Blend

For a background that's alive with wisps of color, consider brush blending your walls. Simply brush on two paint colors at the same time using a crosshatching motion. As you work the colors on the wall, they blend together to create hue variations. You may use low-contrast colors and blend thoroughly for a subtle effect or choose high-contrast hues and blend lightly, leaving bold streaks of color to create a finish that's full of visual movement. The technique requires no precision, and it's nearly impossible to make a mistake. Since each painter applies the paint in a unique way, every room will have a different look. There are two great advantages to using this finish: Blending two colors over a base coat color is a great way to pull together a room's color scheme, and the tone variations help minimize any imperfections in the wall's surface. Whether your room's style is casual or formal, this type of color blending creates a great all-purpose finish that works anywhere.

TIP

Adding paint conditioner to the paint makes it easier to spread and slows drying time, allowing more time to work with a wet edge. You can adjust the ratios of conditioner to paint colors as desired. Experiment on a sample board until you're satisfied with the way the paint blends.

Color Blends

Brush Blend

INSTRUCTIONS

Mask ceiling, baseboards, and trim with painter's tape. Paint the entire wall in the golden yellow base coat color. Paint two coats if necessary. Leave tape on; let the paint dry overnight.

TIP

Semigloss latex paint works best for this technique. Other sheens can be blended but the flatter the sheen the more difficult it is to blend.

Keep in mind that as the colors blend, new hues are created. If you want a hint of green to emerge, for example, blend yellow and blue together.

1

Pour a quart of pink paint into one plastic container and a quart of golden yellow paint into another plastic container. Mix up to 2 tablespoons of paint conditioner into each quart of paint. After experimenting on a sample board, you may decide you need to use more conditioner to achieve easy-flowing color.

2

Dip the trim brush into the pink paint mixture and, working within a 3-foot-square area, apply three to five random crosshatch strokes to the wall.

3

Dip the same brush into the yellow paint mixture and apply over the pink areas in a crosshatch motion, partially blending the yellow into the pink areas.

4

Moving as quickly as possible, begin crosshatching and blending the two colors.

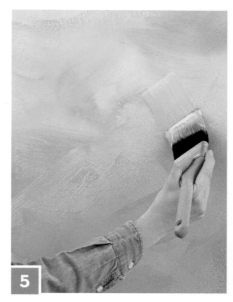

5

Continue to blend adding more of each color as needed to keep the area wet as you work. As you complete one area, move on to an adjacent area and continue to cover one wall without stopping. Let dry.

Variation A

The amount of blending you do will determine the final result. Minimum blending yields high contrast while more blending creates a soft gradation of colors. To create subtle variations of one color such as the range of light blue hues above, pair white with pale blue.

Variation B

To create color variations of lavender with a subtle splash of contrast work with the same basic hue. Choose a medium and a pale value of blue-lavender from one paint sample strip and add a medium value of red-lavender from another paint sample strip.

TIP

As you paint sample boards to explore your color options, try reversing base coat and top coat colors for a dramatic difference in the final result.

The yellow-and-pink color-blended wall features an approximate ratio of 70:30 yellow to pink. The remaining color variations shown are approximately 50:50.

Variation C

Keep in mind that as the colors blend together, new hues are created. If you want a hint of yellow green to emerge, for example, blend yellow, white, blue, and green together. Adding paint conditioner to the paint slows the drying time allowing more time to blend the colors.

Variation D

Try reversing base-coat and top-coat colors for a dramatic difference in the final result. The example above is created by blending light and dark pink hues over a medium pink basecoat. Medium and dark pink blended over a light pink basecoat will yield a completely different result.

Grass Cloth

Grass-cloth wallpaper is a popular element used in many decorating styles. It's available in a wide variety of colors but it can be expensive. If you love the look but not the price tag, you can create a simulation. The technique is painted in 24- to 36-inch-wide panels, reinforcing the appearance of wallpaper. You'll need to set aside a couple of days to complete the technique because alternating panels are painted one day and the remaining panels are completed the following day, but the result is worth the time and effort. The process is similar to painting a woven-fabric technique with two exceptions: Executing the warp and weft patterns in two separate steps rather than at the same time produces a more pronounced textural effect, and using two accent glazes, one light and one dark, simulates the color variations of dyed natural grasses. For alternative color combination ideas, study grass-cloth wallpaper samples and experiment by painting sample boards.

SKILL LEVEL

Intermediate

SPECIAL TOOLS

a. Level with printed ruler

b. Painter's tape

c. Glaze medium

d. Wide wallpaper brush

e. 6-inch-wide paintbrush

a.

b.

c.

d.

e.

TOOLS

Drop cloth

Stir sticks

Paint tray

Two 2-inch tapered trim brushes

Tape measure

Colored pencil

3 plastic containers with printed measurements

Large plastic bucket

Lint-free cotton cloths

PAINT

Semigloss latex for all colors

PALE GOLD FOR BASE COAT

DARK BRICK RED FOR GLAZE COAT

BURGUNDY RED FOR DARK ACCENT GLAZE

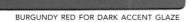
PALE ROSE FOR LIGHT ACCENT GLAZE

Grass Cloth

INSTRUCTIONS

Mask ceiling, baseboards, and trim with painter's tape. Paint the wall the pale gold base-coat color. Paint two coats if necessary. Leave tape on; let paint dry overnight.

The grass-cloth technique is executed in a series of vertical panels. The panels should be narrow enough so you can work comfortably and quickly; a width between 24 and 36 inches is generally manageable. To divide the room into panels of equal width, first measure the total width of each wall in inches. Next divide the total wall width by the desired panel width to determine the number of panels. You can end panels in corners or wrap them around corners, but because maneuvering the wallpaper brush around a corner can be tricky, ending panels in corners is easiest.

Using a plastic container with printed measurements, measure 4 parts glaze to 1 part dark brick red paint into a clean bucket. Mix enough glaze for the entire project so the intensity of the glaze color is consistent from panel to panel. The total amount of glaze mixture should equal the amount of base-coat color applied for one-coat coverage (see page 13). In a second container mix 4 parts glaze to 1 part burgundy red paint. In a third container mix 1 part glaze to 1 part pale rose paint.

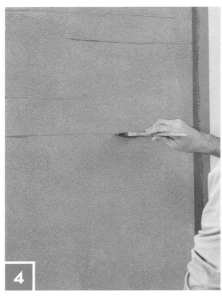

1 To lay out the panels, use a tape measure and colored pencil to measure and mark all the walls with an upper and lower mark for each panel interval.

Use a long level to draw vertical lines from ceiling to baseboard, connecting upper and lower marks at each panel interval. The level will ensure that the lines stay vertical and parallel to one another.

2 Because every other panel is painted the first day and the remaining panels are painted the next day, tape off alternating sections with low-tack painter's tape.

3 Using a trim brush trim with the dark brick red glaze mixture along the ceiling and baseboard of the first taped-off panel. Then use a well-saturated roller to apply glaze to the remainder of the panel. Quickly roll long vertical strokes from ceiling to floor across the entire width of the panel to even out the glaze.

4 Working quickly while the glaze is still wet, use a 2-inch trim brush to apply loose, irregular streaks of the burgundy glaze mixture.

Use a second 2-inch-wide trim brush to quickly apply irregular streaks of the pale rose glaze mixture.

To create the horizontal weave lines, begin at the top left-hand corner of the panel and drag the wallpaper brush across the panel from left to right, applying firm pressure. Drag left-to-right horizontal passes all the way to the bottom of the panel, slightly overlapping the bottom of the previous stroke. Wipe the brush on a damp cloth after each stroke.

Use a 6-inch-wide paintbrush to gently pull through and soften the burgundy and pale rose streaks of glaze mix.

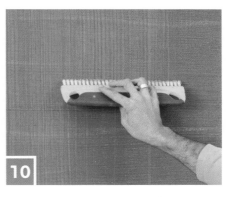

To reinforce the horizontal weave lines, drag the wallpaper brush through the wet glaze again, following Step 6. Repeat the process for each taped-off panel. Leave the tape in place and allow to dry completely.

After the first glaze application is dry, apply another coat of the dark brick red glaze mixture, following Step 3.

For the vertical weave begin at the top left-hand corner of the panel and apply firm pressure as you drag the wallpaper brush straight down to the bottom in one continuous stroke. If you must use a ladder, make a few dry runs to practice stepping down the ladder as you pull the brush through the glaze. Continue vertical passes all the way to the right edge of the panel, slightly overlapping the right edge of the previous stroke. Wipe the brush on a damp cloth after each stroke. Immediately remove the vertical strips of painter's tape. Finish the first series of panels and let them dry overnight. Tape and paint the final series, repeating Steps 2–10. To abut the seams place the tape on top of the dried glaze along the edge where the sections meet.

SKILL LEVEL

Intermediate

SPECIAL TOOLS

a. Standard
   roller frame
   with cover

b. Glaze medium

c. Woodgraining
   tool

d. Lint-free
   cotton cloths

a.

b.

c.

d.

TOOLS

2-inch-wide
low-tack
painter's tape

Drop cloth

Stir sticks

Paint tray

Standard roller
frame with 9-inch
roller cover

2-inch tapered
trim brush

Plastic container
with printed
measurements

Large plastic
bucket

PAINT

Semigloss latex for all colors

PALE GOLD FOR BASE COAT

DARK GOLD FOR GLAZE COAT

Woodgrain Moiré

When you want to include the rustic look of woodgrain in your decorating plans but your color scheme lacks natural wood tones, the faux woodgrain technique is a great alternative. The process employs a special woodgraining tool available at most crafts stores and home centers. The curved and textured rubber tool is pulled downward through a wet top coat of rolled-on glaze mixture using a dragging and rocking motion that creates a grain and knot pattern as it reveals the base coat underneath. This treatment requires a steady, confident hand, so practice is recommended if you're a novice painter. A dark gold hue was used for a glaze coat over a pale gold in the kitchen below. For a very different result, try reversing the base-coat and glaze-coat colors.

INSTRUCTIONS

Mask ceiling, baseboards, and trim with painter's tape. Paint the entire wall in the pale gold base-coat color. Paint two coats if necessary. Leave tape on; let the paint dry overnight.

Using a plastic container with printed measurements, measure 4 parts glaze to 1 part dark gold paint into a clean bucket. Mix enough glaze for the entire project so the intensity of the glaze color is consistent. The total amount of glaze mixture should equal the amount of base-coat color applied for one-coat coverage (see page 13).

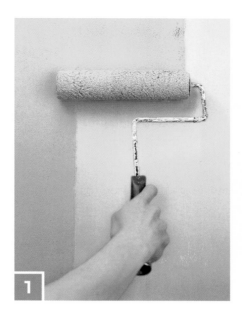

Roll a narrow width of dark gold glaze mixture onto the wall.

Working quickly start at the top and pull the woodgraining tool down the wall, creating a wood "plank" effect. As you pull the tool downward, rock the tool up and down to create the woodgrain texture. Again start at the top, very slightly overlapping the previous "plank," and make another vertical pass adjacent to the first. Continue in this fashion, making a series of planks.

Use a lint-free cotton cloth to clean the excess glaze off the woodgraining tool.

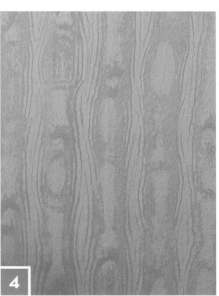

When you have filled the first area with textured "planks," roll on another width of glaze mixture and repeat the process until the entire area is completed. Remove all tape; allow to dry.

Woodgrain Wall Panels

SKILL LEVEL

Intermediate

SPECIAL TOOLS

a. 1- and 2-inch-wide low-tack painter's tape

b. Mini roller

c. Brown gel stain

d. Lint-free cotton cloths

a.

b.

c.

d.

TOOLS

Graph paper

Drop cloth

Stir sticks

Paint tray

Standard roller frame with 9-inch roller cover

2-inch tapered trim brush

Tape measure

Brown color pencil

Level with printed ruler

Mini roller paint tray

Glaze medium

Plastic container with printed measurements

3-inch-wide paintbrush

Polyurethane finish

Faux-painting woodgrain onto walls, furniture, and architectural elements is a time-honored tradition. Throughout history master painters have been highly regarded for their skills in simulating all types of exotic wood species. However you needn't be a master painter to execute woodgrain panels like the ones in the office, opposite. Painting woodgrain on accent panels rather than an entire wall makes the job quick and easy. Using oil-base gel stain for the graining process eliminates the need for combining pigment and solvents because it is premixed. A paintbrush pulled vertically through a coat of wet gel stain makes the fine grain pattern. The bold grain pattern, made by wiping off streaks of gel stain with a soft cloth, creates dramatic contrast. Brushing through the completed grain pattern blends and softens the effect. Use this technique on furniture, raised panels, or any smooth surface that will accept a base coat of color.

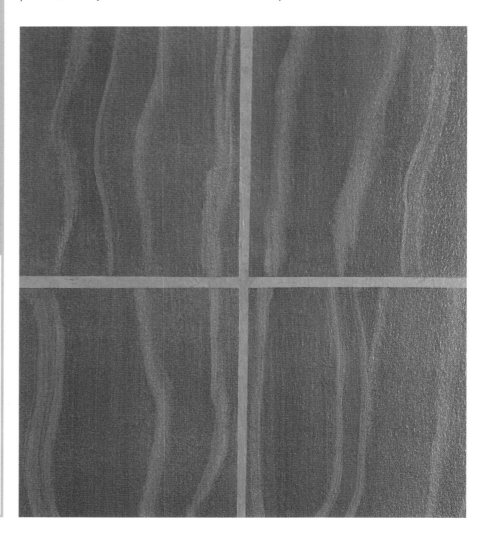

PAINT

Semigloss latex for all colors

TERRA-COTTA FOR BASE COAT

MEDIUM GRAY FOR BORDER BASE COAT

DARK GRAY FOR BORDER GLAZE COAT

Woodgrain Wall Panels

INSTRUCTIONS

Mask ceiling, baseboards, and trim with painter's tape. Paint the entire wall in the terra-cotta base-coat color. Paint two coats if necessary. Leave tape on; let the paint dry overnight.

Using a plastic container with printed measurements, measure and mix 4 parts glaze to 1 part dark gray paint.

To divide a section of the wall into square panels, first measure the total height and width of the wall in inches. Draw a sketch on graph paper to help you visualize panel sizes. The four panels shown are 24 inches square. To lay out the panels, use the tape measure and colored pencil to measure and mark the wall with an upper and lower mark for each vertical line. Use the long level and colored pencil to draw vertical lines to connect the upper and lower marks at each interval. The level will ensure that the lines stay vertical and parallel to one another. Measure and mark the wall for horizontal lines in the same manner. Use the 1-inch-wide low-tack painter's tape to tape off the panels.

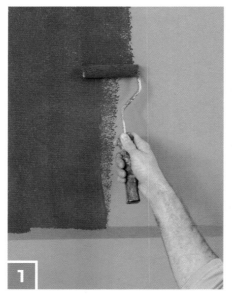

1

Pour brown gel stain into the mini roller paint tray. Saturate the mini roller and roll a thin, even coat of stain onto one panel.

2

Use the 3-inch-wide paintbrush and apply firm pressure to pull down through the gel stain from top to bottom in long, straight strokes. This creates a streaked effect that simulates fine woodgrain.

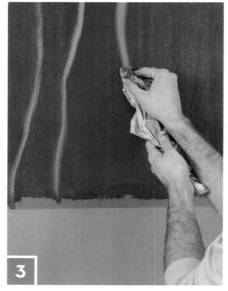

3

To create the bold grain lines, loosely fold a piece of soft, lint-free cloth. Starting at the top of the panel, pull the folded cloth down toward the bottom of the panel to remove most of the gel stain in a wide streak, exposing the base-coat color. The streaks should not be straight but should have gentle curves. To do this roll the folded cloth gently from side to side as you pull downward.

4

Use the 6-inch-wide paintbrush to gently brush through the gel stain, softening the bold grain lines. Make straight top-to-bottom strokes and use very gentle pressure. Complete all four panels, one at a time. Let dry then remove all tape.

5 To create the borders between the woodgrain panels, use the 2-inch-wide painter's tape to tape off the inside panel edges.

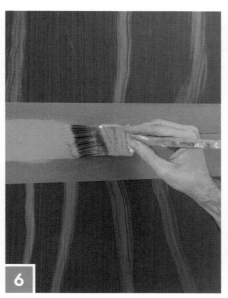

6 Use the 2-inch tapered trim brush to base-coat the borders with medium gray paint. Let dry.

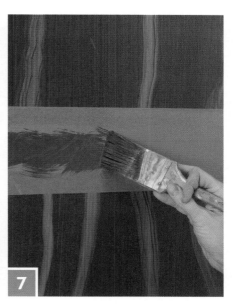

7 Use the 2-inch tapered trim brush to apply a thin coat of dark gray glaze.

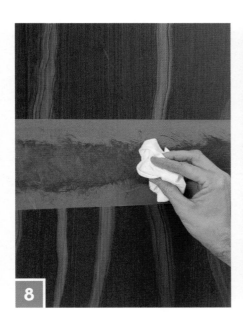

8 Use a small bunched piece of damp cloth to gently dab and soften the dark gray glaze, creating a mottled effect.

9 Immediately remove all tape and let dry. To enhance the depth of the gel stain and bring out the simulated woodgrain, tape off the outside edges of the panel grouping, then apply one or two coats of polyurethane finish, letting the varnish dry between coats. Let dry and remove all tape.

Wicker

Casual and timeless wicker furnishings and accents impart a relaxed feeling to a room's decor. That same ambience is captured with the faux wicker paint treatment in the bedroom, opposite. To make the process easy the wicker technique is executed in strips or panels. Pulling two sizes of homemade combs, made from squeegees, through two top-coat glaze layers simulates the warp and weft pattern found in woven wicker. To make the combs use a crafts knife to cut notches along the squeegees' rubber blades. One squeegee gets wider notches than the other. When used in combination, a basket-weave pattern is created. Neutral hues that mimic wicker's natural tones give the most realistic results. Use a light color for the glaze mixture and a darker color for the base coat.

SKILL LEVEL

Intermediate

SPECIAL TOOLS

a. 2-inch-wide low-tack painter's tape

b. 2 squeegees

c. Crafts knife

d. Glaze medium

a.

b.

c.

d.

TOOLS

Drop cloth

Stir sticks

Paint tray

Standard roller frame with 9-inch roller cover

2-inch tapered trim brush

Tape measure

Level with printed ruler

Tan color pencil

Ruler

Fine-tip marker

Self-healing cutting mat

Plastic container with printed measurements

Large plastic bucket

Lint-free cotton cloths

PAINT

Semigloss latex for all colors

MEDIUM GOLD FOR BASE COAT

ANTIQUE WHITE FOR GLAZE COAT

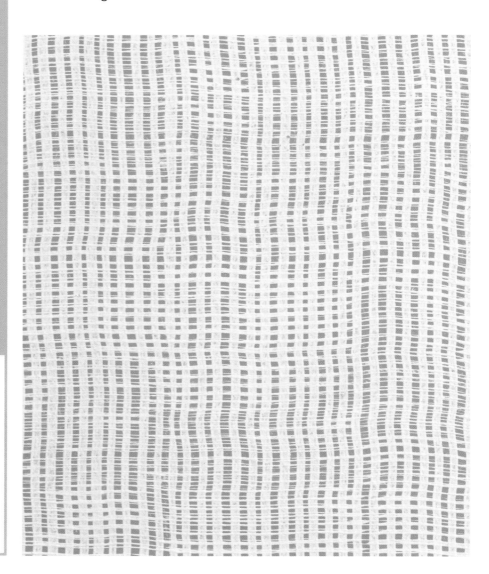

Wicker

INSTRUCTIONS

Mask ceiling, baseboards, and trim with painter's tape. Paint the entire wall in the medium gold base-coat color. Paint two coats if necessary. Leave tape on; let the paint dry overnight.

The wicker technique is executed in a series of vertical panels. The panels should be narrow enough in width so you can work comfortably and quickly; a width between 24 and 36 inches is generally manageable. To divide the room into panels of equal width, first measure the total width of each wall in inches. Next divide the total wall width by the desired panel width to determine the number of panels. Plan your layout to have panels end in corners.

Using a plastic container with printed measurements, measure 4 parts glaze to 1 part antique white paint into a clean bucket. Mix enough glaze for the entire project so the intensity of the glaze color is consistent from panel to panel. The total amount of glaze mixture should equal the amount of base-coat color applied for one-coat coverage (see page 13).

To prepare the squeegees use a ruler and fine-tip marker to mark the blade of one squeegee in ⅛-inch-wide sections. Working on a safe cutting surface, such as a self-healing cutting mat, cut out every other section with a crafts knife. A little variance in the notches is acceptable. Repeat the process on the other squeegee, making the sections 1⁄16-inch wide or as small as possible.

1 To lay out the panels, use a tape measure and colored pencil to measure and mark all the walls with an upper and lower mark for each panel interval. Then use a long level to draw in vertical lines from ceiling to baseboard, connecting upper and lower marks at each panel interval. The level will ensure that the lines stay vertical and parallel to one another.

2 Because every other panel is painted the first day and the remaining panels are painted the next day, tape off alternating sections with low-tack painter's tape.

3 Using a trim brush trim with the glaze mixture along the ceiling and baseboard of the first taped-off panel, then use a well-saturated roller to apply glaze to the remainder of the panel. Quickly roll long vertical strokes from ceiling to floor across the entire width of the panel to even out the glaze.

4

To create the vertical weave lines, begin at the top left-hand corner of the panel and, applying firm pressure, pull the wide-notch squeegee straight down to the bottom of the panel in one continuous stroke. Try to complete one run without stopping. If you must stop begin again slowly. Minimal flaws are acceptable. Drag top-to-bottom all the way to the right edge of the panel, using the edge of the previous stroke as a guide until the entire panel is textured. Wipe the squeegee on a damp cloth after each stroke. Repeat the process for each taped-off panel. Leave the tape in place and allow to dry completely.

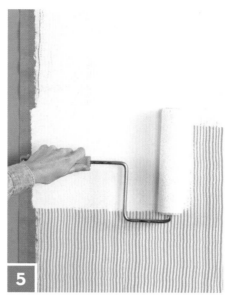

5

Roll the glaze mixture over the section, covering the vertical texture lines.

6

To create the horizontal weave lines, begin at the top left-hand corner of the panel and pull the narrow-notch squeegee across the panel from left to right, through the glaze. Drag left-to-right horizontal passes all the way to the bottom of the panel, using the edge of the previous stroke as a guide until the entire panel is textured. Wipe the squeegee on a damp cloth after each stroke.

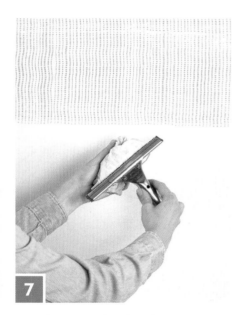

7

Wipe the excess glaze from the squeegee after each stroke.

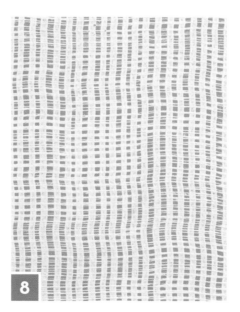

8

Complete the first series of panels and let them dry overnight before taping and painting the final series, repeating Steps 3–7. To abut the seams place the tape on top of the dried glaze along the edge where the sections meet.

TIP

When combing through the glaze, start slowly and keep a light but firm pressure on the squeegee. Glaze is slippery, and if the pressure on the squeegee is too firm, it will slide around. If this happens reroll the glaze and start the panel again.

SPECIAL TOOLS

a. ½-inch-wide drafting tape

b. Glaze medium

c. Mini roller

d. Round artist's brush

a.

b.

c.

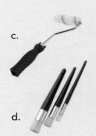

d.

TOOLS

Drop cloth

Stir sticks

Paint tray

Standard roller frame with 9-inch roller cover

2-inch tapered trim brush

Level with printed ruler

3 plastic containers with printed measurements

3 mini roller paint trays

Absorbent paper towels

Soft lint-free cloths

3-gallon bucket

Paper towels

PAINT

Semigloss latex for all colors

BEIGE FOR BASE COAT AND GLAZE COAT

PALE GRAY FOR GLAZE COAT

IVORY FOR HIGHLIGHTS

DARK GRAY FOR FINAL GLAZE AND MORTAR

Brick

The classic look of light-color brick imparts a loft-style look to plain walls in the living room, opposite. This technique takes a little time to accomplish because it requires a closely taped-off grid pattern followed by several layers of glaze to create a realistic effect. Specialty ½-inch-wide drafting tape, available at art supply retailers, forms the mortar lines. Three rolled-on glaze-and-paint layers create a random pattern of colors and simulate the tones in natural brick. Casual freehand painting accentuates the mortar lines and completes the look. Whether you use it below a chair rail, to frame a fireplace, or to enhance an accent wall, this faux-brick paint effect works well with casual, rustic, or retro decorating styles. For a traditional red brick palette, try rust and tan glaze mixes over a dark peach base coat and use dark gray or dark brown for the mortar lines.

Brick

INSTRUCTIONS

Mask ceiling, baseboards, and trim with painter's tape. Paint the entire wall in the beige base-coat color. Paint two coats if necessary. Leave tape on; let the paint dry overnight.

Use a plastic container with printed measurements to mix 4 parts glaze to 1 part pale gray paint. In a second plastic container, mix 4 parts glaze to 1 part beige paint. In a third plastic container, mix 4 parts glaze to 1 part dark gray paint.

Fill a 3-gallon bucket half full of clean water for rinsing cloths.

Tape off long rows approximately 3 inches apart on the entire wall from ceiling to floor. These may be taped without measuring but check periodically with a level to keep them reasonably level. Some unevenness occurs but gives a natural appearance. If you desire measure and mark 3-inch intervals, then draw lines using the level before taping.

Tape off vertical divisions for individual bricks. The strips of tape should not be perfectly straight but slightly angled for a more natural appearance. The bricks should vary in length from 6 to 8 inches. Offset the tape strips to indicate staggered rows of bricks.

Pour some of the pale gray glaze mixture into the mini roller paint tray and lightly load the mini roller with glaze. After rolling the paint roller across a stack of absorbent paper towels to remove some of the paint, lightly roll the glaze onto the wall, allowing the roller to skip as you roll in order to create a random pattern of coverage. Let dry.

Pour some of the beige glaze mixture into a mini roller tray. Lightly load the mini roller with glaze and skip-roll the glaze onto the wall as in Step 3. Let dry.

Pour ivory paint into a clean mini roller tray, lightly load the mini roller, and skip-roll the paint onto the wall as in Step 3. Let dry.

6

Remove all of the tape.

7

Pour some of the dark gray glaze mixture into a clean mini roller tray. Lightly load the mini roller with glaze and skip-roll the glaze onto a 2-foot-square irregularly shaped section of the wall.

8

Working quickly while the glaze is still wet, dampen a piece of lint-free cloth with water and wring it out thoroughly so that it is only slightly damp. Loosely bunch the cloth and begin to dab and smudge the wet glaze mixture to remove some of the glaze and create a mottled appearance. Working one area at a time, finish glazing the wall. As the cloth becomes saturated with glaze, rinse and wring it out again. Let glaze dry.

9

To add depth and realism to the effect, use a round artist's brush to apply the dark gray glaze mixture onto the mortar lines. As you brush on the glaze, let the brush skip and create irregular coverage. Let dry.

10

After the wall is complete, stand back and evaluate the effect. If there are areas that need more work, retape sections and apply glaze mixtures to balance the colors and reinforce dark areas or light areas as needed.

TIP

Explore your color options by painting sample boards. Try reversing base-coat and top-coat colors for a dramatic difference in the final result.

Study different types and colors of natural brick to get ideas for color combinations you like.

Limestone Blocks

SKILL LEVEL

Intermediate

SPECIAL TOOLS

a. Low-tack painter's tape

b. Glaze medium

c. Mini roller

d. Stippling brush

a.

b.

c.

d.

TOOLS

Drop cloth

Stir sticks

Paint tray

Standard roller frame with 9-inch roller cover

2-inch tapered trim brush

Graph paper

Tape measure

Tan color pencil

Level with printed ruler

3 plastic containers with printed measurements

Mini roller paint tray

Soft lint-free cloths

3-gallon bucket

PAINT

Semigloss latex for all colors

ANTIQUE WHITE FOR BASE COAT AND HIGHLIGHTS

DARK GRAY FOR GLAZE COAT

PALE GOLD FOR GLAZE COAT

Sandy gold colors enhanced with earthy gray and antique white combine in a muted palette to create the serene backdrop of limestone blocks in the bathroom below. The process is not difficult but requires a little time to complete. It begins with a grid of horizontal blocks marked on the wall in staggered rows. The size of blocks you use is up to you. Because the process requires several layers of glaze and retaping blocks at the final stages, a large block pattern can be painted nearly as quickly as a small one. Whether you choose to paint large blocks or small ones, the painting process yields unique visual characteristics on each block. Because the color variations are subtle and the palette neutral, this technique works well in full-size rooms because it will not overpower furnishings and it complements casual as well as formal decor.

INSTRUCTIONS

Mask ceiling, baseboards, and trim with painter's tape. Paint the entire wall in the antique white base-coat color. Paint two coats if necessary. Leave tape on; let the paint dry overnight.

Use a plastic container with printed measurements to mix 4 parts glaze to 1 part dark gray paint. In a second plastic container, mix 4 parts glaze to 1 part pale gold paint. In a third plastic container, mix 4 parts glaze to 1 part antique white paint.

To divide the wall into blocks, measure the total height and width of the wall in inches. Draw a sketch on graph paper to help you visualize block sizes. The blocks shown are 8×10-inch rectangles, placed horizontally. To begin laying out the panels, use the tape measure and colored pencil to measure and mark the wall at intervals for the horizontal lines. Use the long level and colored pencil to draw in horizontal lines. The level will ensure that the lines stay horizontal and parallel to one another. Then, using the level, measure and mark the wall for each vertical line. Be sure to stagger the vertical lines.

Because alternating blocks are painted first and allowed to dry before adjacent blocks are painted, tape off alternating blocks with the low-tack painter's tape.

Fill a 3-gallon bucket half full of clean water for rinsing cloths.

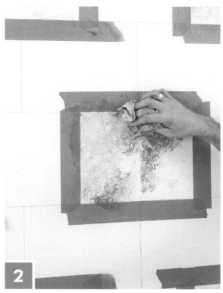

Pour some of the dark gray glaze mixture into the mini paint roller tray and lightly load the mini roller with glaze. Lightly roll the glaze onto the wall, allowing the roller to skip as you roll in order to create a random pattern of coverage.

Working quickly while the glaze is still wet, dampen a piece of lint-free cloth with water and wring it out thoroughly so that it is only slightly damp. Loosely bunch the cloth and begin to dab and smudge the wet glaze mixture to remove some of the glaze and create a mottled appearance. Working one block at a time, finish glazing the blocks. As the cloth becomes saturated with glaze, rinse and wring it out again. Let the glaze dry.

Pour some of the pale gold glaze mixture into the mini roller tray and lightly load the mini roller with glaze. Lightly roll the glaze onto the wall, allowing the roller to skip as you roll in order to create a random pattern of coverage.

Working quickly while the glaze is still wet, pounce with a stippling brush or large soft-bristle paintbrush to create an overall even, softly mottled effect. Let dry.

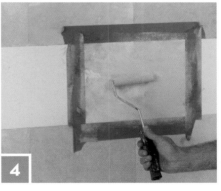

Once you have established an overall look for the blocks using the dark gray and pale gold glaze mixtures, create highlight areas where some blocks adjoin others. To do this pour some of the antique white glaze mixture into the mini roller tray and lightly load the mini roller with glaze. Lightly roll the glaze onto the chosen block along the taped edges or in corners where highlights are desired. Be sure to allow the roller to skip as you roll to create a random pattern. Lightly soften and blend the glaze with the damp cloth. After the wall is complete, stand back and evaluate the effect. If there are areas that need more work, retape sections and apply glaze mixtures to balance the colors and reinforce dark areas or light areas as needed.

Irregular Stone Blocks

A weathered-stone paint treatment gives the decorative ledge in the two-story entryway below character and imparts a warm natural feel to the space. The casually executed technique requires only a few simple steps and encourages creativity in that no two painters will create stones that look alike. Several layers of acrylic paint colors sponged on randomly over a taped-off pattern of irregular-size rectangles give each stone its unique look. Casual handpainting along the mortar lines after the tape is removed completes the effect. Use this technique to add drama and rustic charm to fireplace surrounds, above or below chair rails, or even on the floor. On a sample board experiment with color combinations that not only mimic nature but also complement your room's color scheme.

SKILL LEVEL
Intermediate

SPECIAL TOOLS
a. 1-inch-wide painter's tape
b. Paper plates
c. Assorted artist's brushes
d. Natural sponge

a.

b.

c.

d.

TOOLS
Drop cloth

Stir sticks

Paint tray

Standard roller frame with 9-inch roller cover

2-inch tapered trim brush

PAINT
Semigloss latex for base coat, acrylic crafts paint for all others

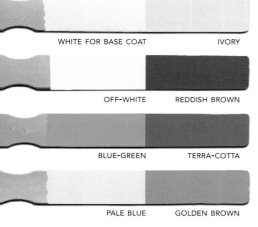

WHITE FOR BASE COAT	IVORY
OFF-WHITE	REDDISH BROWN
BLUE-GREEN	TERRA-COTTA
PALE BLUE	GOLDEN BROWN

INSTRUCTIONS

Mask ceiling, baseboards, and trim with painter's tape. Paint the entire wall in the white base-coat color. Paint two coats if necessary. Leave tape on; let the paint dry overnight.

Tape off an irregular pattern of rectangles and squares. These are between 4 and 14 inches wide. Try to make tape lines perpendicular but work without a level; slight irregularities will create a more realistic look.

Pour a puddle of each acrylic crafts paint onto a disposable plate. Wet and wring out a small natural sponge. Dip the sponge into the ivory and begin to randomly apply the paint to a few of the taped-off spaces using a light dabbing motion. Then, without cleaning the sponge, pick up darker colors randomly and apply to the wet "stones," allowing the colors to blend slightly. Make some of them darker, some lighter, and some greener or bluer. Rinse the sponge and repeat the process until all of the taped-off rectangles are filled with dappled color. Stand back to view your work, looking for a balance of colors. Make adjustments as needed.

Remove all tape and let the paint dry thoroughly.

Using a round artist's brush, paint rounded corners and irregular edges on each stone block using off-white, golden brown, and terra-cotta as needed to create a variety of hues. Do not rinse the brush between colors but let the hues mingle and blend naturally.

Use a small piece of sponge to lightly sponge over the rounded corners and stone edges using off-white, then golden brown, and finally terra-cotta.

Use a round artist's brush to paint the mortar between the stones with ivory, off-white, and golden brown. Don't mix the colors; leave them a little streaky to enhance the aged appearance.

Marble

Marbleizing is one of the more popular faux-finish techniques. In the past it required many steps and numerous layers of applied paint and glaze combinations. Now, due to an innovative method, realistic results can be achieved in a few steps. The unique process makes use of heavy plastic brushed with paint to apply color on the base-coat surface and create a marble pattern at the same time. Generally two layers of color are applied using the plastic followed by handpainting vein lines. A glaze-and-paint top coat softens and unifies the colors. Extra layers of pattern and unifying washes may be applied to add depth if desired. Practice this technique first on sample boards to gain a feel for working with the paint and plastic. Whether you execute this marble technique on architectural details such as corbels, columns, and raised panels or to decorate furniture pieces, it creates an elegant addition to any room.

SKILL LEVEL

Intermediate

SPECIAL TOOLS

a. Glaze medium

b. Chip brushes

c. Plastic drop cloth

a.

b.

c.

TOOLS

2-inch-wide low-tack painter's tape

Drop cloth

Stir sticks

Paint tray

Standard roller frame with 9-inch roller cover

2-inch tapered trim brush

3 plastic containers with printed measurements

Scissors

Artist's liner brush

PAINT

Semigloss latex for all colors

IVORY FOR BASE COAT AND GLAZE COAT

TAUPE FOR GLAZE COAT

GRAY FOR GLAZE COAT

Marble

INSTRUCTIONS

Mask ceiling, baseboards, and trim with painter's tape. Paint the entire wall in the ivory base-coat color. Paint two coats if necessary. Leave tape on; let the paint dry overnight.

Use a plastic container with printed measurements to mix 4 parts glaze to 1 part taupe paint. In a second plastic container, mix 4 parts glaze to 1 part gray paint. In a third plastic container, mix 4 parts glaze to 1 part ivory paint.

With scissors cut two pieces of plastic to about 18×24 inches.

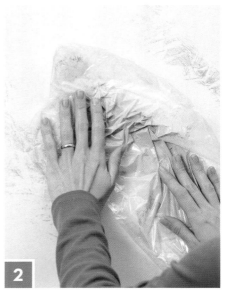

Dip a 2-inch-wide chip brush into the taupe glaze mixture and brush onto one of the 18×24-inch sheets of plastic. When applying the paint to the plastic, brush it on evenly and thinly to avoid dripping and long drying times between layers of paint.

Lay the plastic on the base-coat surface with the paint side down, allowing the plastic to cling to the surface and create random shapes and lines. Peel off the plastic and place it onto a new surface area. You'll get about three applications before you'll need to reload the plastic with paint. Let dry.

Brush gray glaze mixture onto the second 18×24-inch sheet of plastic and repeat Steps 1 and 2. Overlap the taupe areas in some places. Let dry.

Once you've covered the area sufficiently with the plastic-imprinted patterns, use an artist's liner brush to add basic vein lines, connecting the shapes with the appropriate color. For example connect the taupe shapes with taupe veins and the gray shapes with gray veins. Vary the line widths by changing the pressure on your brush. Begin vein lines where the marble pattern has already been established, then move to open areas and connect to other established areas. Let dry thoroughly.

5

Use a 3-inch-wide chip brush to sparingly brush ivory glaze mix onto the wall to soften the marble effect and unify the colors. Work quickly and pat the glaze mixture using a piece of bunched-up plastic to blend the glaze and avoid harsh start-and-stop lines as the glaze dries.

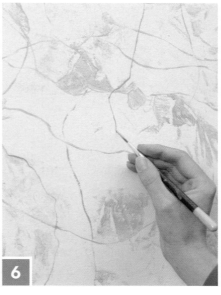

6

Accentuate the previously painted vein lines by retracing them with their original color and add more vein lines as desired. Vary the thickness of the vein lines and use all hues in the color scheme.

TIP

The flow of the grain is critical to the overall success of a marbleizing project. Bolder lines should follow a directional flow while smaller, finer veins may branch in various directions.

Add depth by building more layers of color. Accent colors applied with the plastic, as well as tints of the accent colors applied in thinned glazes, can further enhance the final effect.

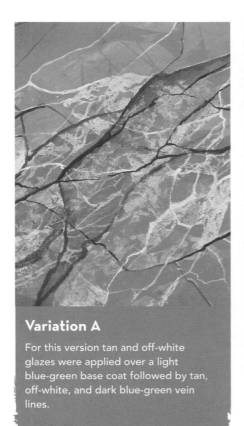

Variation A

For this version tan and off-white glazes were applied over a light blue-green base coat followed by tan, off-white, and dark blue-green vein lines.

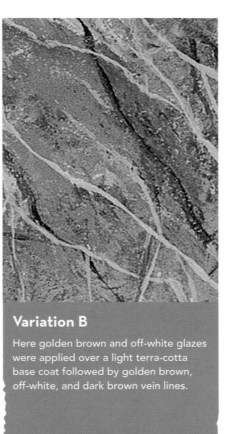

Variation B

Here golden brown and off-white glazes were applied over a light terra-cotta base coat followed by golden brown, off-white, and dark brown vein lines.

TIP

Explore your color options by painting sample boards. Try reversing base-coat and top-coat colors for a dramatic difference in the final result.

Look at different types of marble and study both the graining and coloring of the natural stone.

SKILL LEVEL

Beginner

SPECIAL TOOLS

a. Level with printed ruler

b. 2-inch-wide low-tack painter's tape

c. Glaze medium

d. Mini roller

e. Plastic drop cloth

a.

b.

c.

d.

e.

TOOLS

Tape measure

Green color pencil

Drop cloth

Stir sticks

Standard paint tray

Standard roller frame with 9-inch roller cover

2-inch tapered trim brush

2 plastic containers with printed measurements

2 mini roller paint trays

PAINT

Semigloss latex for all colors

DARK COPPER METALLIC FOR BASE COAT

GREEN METALLIC FOR GLAZE COAT

TURQUOISE FOR GLAZE COAT

Copper Verdigris

The intriguing aged blue-green patina found on antique copper architectural elements is re-created on the decorative framed panel above the fireplace shown below. The finish looks complicated but is actually simple to accomplish. Two colors of blue-green glaze rolled over a copper base coat and textured with plastic create the visual dimension. A simple frame made from picture frame molding completes the look. Use this technique in small areas to complement copper architectural elements, on recessed panels, or on small wall areas where a focal point is desired. For additional depth layer on glaze coats in different copper metallic paint colors and texture with plastic as above.

INSTRUCTIONS

To lay out the panel, use the tape measure and colored pencil to measure and mark the wall with an upper and lower mark for each vertical line. Use the long level and colored pencil to draw in vertical lines to connect the upper and lower marks at each interval. The level will ensure that the lines stay vertical and parallel to one another. Use the tape measure and colored pencil to measure and mark the wall for each horizontal line. Use the long level and colored pencil to draw in horizontal lines to complete the rectangle. You will need to design your rectangle to fit your space. The one shown here is 28×42 inches. Tape off the rectangle with low-tack painter's tape.

Using a plastic container with printed measurements, measure equal parts glaze and green metallic paint. In another container mix equal parts glaze and turquoise paint. Pour some of the green metallic glaze mixture and turquoise glaze mixture into separate mini paint trays.

Cut a piece of 1-mil plastic drop cloth to about twice the size of your rectangle.

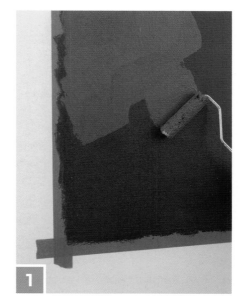

1 Base-coat the rectangle with dark copper metallic paint. Paint two coats if necessary. Leave the tape on; let the paint dry. Next roll the green metallic glaze mixture onto the rectangle using light pressure as you roll to allow some of the base-coat color to show through.

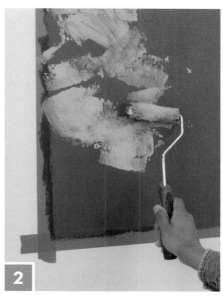

2 Quickly add some of the turquoise glaze mixture, covering about 60 to 70 percent of the rectangle. Turn the roller and lift using light pressure as you roll to allow some of the base coat color to show through and create a random pattern.

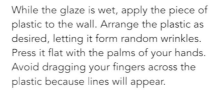

3 While the glaze is wet, apply the piece of plastic to the wall. Arrange the plastic as desired, letting it form random wrinkles. Press it flat with the palms of your hands. Avoid dragging your fingers across the plastic because lines will appear.

Starting at the top left-hand corner, peel the plastic off. Avoid dragging the plastic through the wet glaze. Remove tape and let dry.

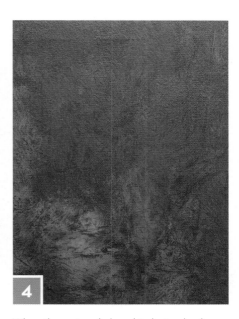

4 When the rectangle has dried, step back and evaluate the result. If some areas need more green metallic or copper colors, retape and apply the desired color glaze mixture, then blot and blend with a piece of scrunched-up plastic.

SPECIAL TOOLS

a. Level with printed ruler

b. 2-inch-wide low-tack painter's tape

c. Glaze medium

d. 6-inch-wide paintbrush

a.

b.

c.

d.

TOOLS

Drop cloth

Stir sticks

Standard-size paint trays

Standard roller frame with 9-inch roller cover

2-inch tapered trim brush

Tape measure

Light-color pencil

2 plastic containers with printed measurements

Graph paper

Brushed Stainless Steel

The softly brushed finish of gleaming stainless steel is a perfect accompaniment to contemporary decorating style. Two layers of metallic paint-and-glaze mixtures, one pewter and one silver, applied over a dark base coat simulate the industrial look of stainless-steel panels on the accent wall shown below. Using a wide paintbrush to sweep on the glaze mixtures creates the brushed-metal effect. The block size used determines the final appearance. Large rectangles are dramatic and expansive while small rectangles create an energetic effect. When planning your rectangle layout, take artwork and furniture into consideration.

PAINT

Semigloss latex for all colors

BLACK FOR BASE COAT

PEWTER METALLIC FOR GLAZE COAT

SILVER METALLIC FOR GLAZE COAT

INSTRUCTIONS

Mask ceiling, baseboards, and trim with painter's tape. Paint the entire wall in the black base-coat color. Paint two coats if necessary. Leave tape on; let the paint dry overnight.

To divide the wall into horizontal blocks, first measure the total height and width of the wall in inches. Draw a sketch on graph paper to help you visualize block sizes. The blocks shown are 24×38 inches.

Using a plastic container with printed measurements, measure equal parts glaze and pewter metallic paint. In another container mix equal parts glaze and silver metallic paint. Mix enough glaze for the entire project so the intensity of the glaze color is consistent. The total amount of glaze mixture should equal the amount of base-coat color applied for one-coat coverage (see page 13).

To begin laying out the panels, use the tape measure and colored pencil to measure and mark the wall with an upper and lower mark for each vertical line. Use the long level and colored pencil to draw vertical lines to connect the upper and lower marks at each interval. The level will ensure that the lines stay vertical and parallel to one another. Use the tape measure and colored pencil to measure and mark the wall at intervals for the horizontal lines. Use the long level and colored pencil to draw in horizontal lines to complete the block pattern.

Because alternating blocks are painted first and allowed to dry before adjacent blocks are painted, tape off alternating blocks with low-tack painter's tape.

Pour some pewter metallic paint and silver metallic paint into separate paint trays. Dip the 6-inch-wide brush into the pewter glaze mixture, then dab off the excess onto the upper portion of the paint tray. Using long, sweeping, straight strokes, horizontally brush the glaze over the rectangle. Let some of the base-coat color show through and create long streaks of color. Leave a bit of the black edge showing in some spots along the taped edges of the rectangle. Complete all taped off squares and let dry.

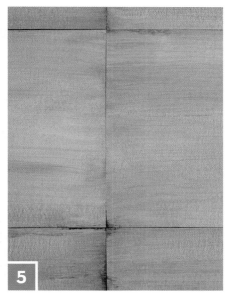

Using long, sweeping, straight strokes, horizontally brush the silver metallic glaze mixture over the rectangle. Let some of the black base coat and pewter glaze color show through and create long streaks of color. Remove the tape and let dry.

Tape off adjacent rectangles and brush on the pewter, then silver glaze mixtures, repeating Steps 3 and 4. When all the rectangles have been painted, step back and evaluate the result. If some rectangles need more pewter or silver glaze colors, retape and adjust as needed. Remove tape and let dry.

SKILL LEVEL

Beginner

SPECIAL TOOLS

a. Glaze medium

b. 6-inch-wide brush

a.

b.

TOOLS

2-inch-wide low-tack painter's tape

Drop cloth

Stir sticks

Paint trays

Standard roller frame with 9-inch roller cover

2-inch tapered trim brush

2 plastic containers with printed measurements

PAINT

Semigloss latex for all colors

PALE GOLD FOR BASE COAT

PALE GOLD METALLIC FOR GLAZE COAT

BRIGHT GOLD METALLIC FOR GLAZE COAT

Brushed Gold

Nothing makes a striking statement in a room's decor like the soft glimmer of metallic finishes on walls or furnishings. The living room shown below demonstrates how two colors of gold metallic glaze mixtures, one pale and one bright, combine to impart a rich patina reminiscent of aged brushed metal. The width of the paintbrush used and the amount of blending determine the final result. This wall was painted with a 6-inch-wide paintbrush doing very little blending. A wide variety of gold metallic paint hues is available from paint centers and online. Purchase small samples and experiment on sample boards to determine the combination you prefer. Use this technique in either formal or contemporary spaces for a very dramatic effect.

INSTRUCTIONS

Mask ceiling, baseboards, and trim with painter's tape. Paint the entire wall in the pale gold base-coat color. Paint two coats if necessary. Leave tape on; let the paint dry overnight.

Using a plastic container with printed measurements, measure equal parts glaze and pale gold metallic paint. In another container mix equal parts glaze and bright gold metallic paint. Mix enough glaze for the entire project so the intensity of the glaze color is consistent. The total amount of glaze mixture should equal the amount of base-coat color applied for one-coat coverage (see page 13).

1

Pour some of each glaze mixture into separate paint trays that are wide enough to accommodate the 6-inch-wide paintbrush. Dip the paintbrush into the pale gold glaze mixture and, using large X strokes, begin to block in an irregularly shaped section of wall approximately 28 inches square.

2

Without cleaning the brush dip into the bright gold glaze mixture and, using large X strokes, blend with the pale gold glaze mixture. The amount of dark gold you apply is optional. This wall shows approximately 50 percent pale gold and 50 percent bright gold.

3

Begin lightly blending the two colors of gold metallic glaze, dipping into each glaze mix as necessary.

4

After filling in a large area, but before the paint has completely dried, go back over the area, adding pale gold glaze mixture and bright gold glaze mixture and blending until the desired result is achieved.

5

For a smooth, low-contrast look, blend the glaze mixtures thoroughly. For a high-contrast look, shown opposite, only lightly blend the colors together. Long, large brushstrokes make the most striking patterns in the metallic paint, but work the glazes until you are happy with them. Remove tape; allow the glazes to dry.

SKILL LEVEL

Intermediate

SPECIAL TOOLS

a. Level with printed ruler

b. 2-inch-wide low-tack painter's tape

c. Two mini roller trays

d. Two mini roller frames with mini rollers

a.

b.

c.

d.

TOOLS

Drop cloth

Stir sticks

Standard-size paint tray

Standard roller frame with 9-inch roller cover

2-inch tapered trim brush

Graph paper

Tape measure

Light-color pencil

PAINT

Semigloss latex for all colors

DARK COPPER METALLIC FOR BASE COAT

BRIGHT COPPER METALLIC FOR TOP COAT

PALE COPPER METALLIC FOR TOP COAT

Copper Blocks

A pattern of square blocks rendered in three colors of copper metallic paint applied over a copper-hue base coat creates the impression of elegant metal leaf on the dining room wall shown below. Mini rollers are employed to apply the paints, and varying pressure is used during the rolling process to achieve a hit-or-miss effect. The result is a unique pattern of copper hues on each block. Use this treatment for a focal-point wall in a living room or dining room or try it as a wainscot in a master bath, where the metallic effect and warm color would combine well with dark wood vanities.

INSTRUCTIONS

Mask ceiling, baseboards, and trim with painter's tape. Paint the entire wall in the dark copper metallic base-coat color. Paint two coats if necessary. Leave tape on; let the paint dry overnight.

To divide the wall into blocks, first measure the total height and width of the wall in inches. Draw a sketch on graph paper to help you visualize block sizes. The blocks shown are 14 inches square.

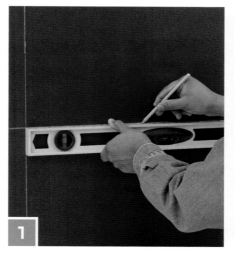

To begin laying out the blocks, use the tape measure and colored pencil to measure and mark the wall with an upper and lower mark for each vertical line. Use the long level and colored pencil to draw in vertical lines to connect the upper and lower marks at each interval. The level will ensure that the lines stay vertical and parallel to one another. Use the tape measure and colored pencil to measure and mark the wall at intervals for the horizontal lines. Use the long level and colored pencil to draw in horizontal lines to complete the block pattern.

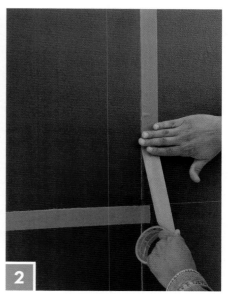

Because alternating blocks are painted first and allowed to dry before adjacent blocks are painted, tape off alternating blocks with low-tack painter's tape.

Pour pale copper metallic paint and bright copper metallic paint into separate mini roller paint trays. Begin by rolling the bright copper paint onto one square at a time. Turn the roller and lift using light pressure as you roll to allow some of the base-coat color to show through and create a random pattern.

Roll pale copper paint onto each square, allowing some of the base coat and bright copper paint to show through. Again use light pressure and turn the roller and lift as you roll to create a random pattern. Complete all taped-off squares. Remove tape and let dry.

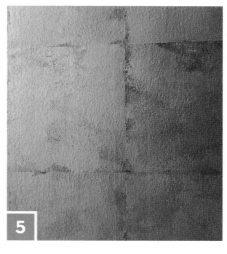

Tape off adjacent squares and repeat Steps 3 and 4 to complete the remaining blocks. Remove the tape and let dry. When all the squares have been painted, step back and evaluate the result. If some squares need more bright or pale copper color, retape and adjust as needed. To make one square stand out against an adjacent square, tape off only one or two sides and add the needed color against the taped line. Remove tape and let dry.

SKILL LEVEL

Intermediate

SPECIAL TOOLS

a. Large putty knife

b. Wallpaper paste brush

c. Pearlescent glaze medium

d. Mini roller with 6-inch roller cover

e. Lint-free cotton cloths

a.

b.

c.

d.

e.

TOOLS

2-inch-wide low-tack painter's tape

Drop cloth

Untinted Venetian plaster compound

Stir sticks

Standard paint tray

Standard roller frame with 9-inch roller cover

2-inch tapered trim brush

Plastic container with printed measurements

2 large plastic buckets

PAINT

Semigloss latex for both colors

PERIWINKLE BLUE FOR BASE COAT

PURPLE FOR GLAZE COAT

Pearl Wash

A cool blue base coat and a wash of vibrant purple paint mixed with pearlescent glaze medium applied over a base of troweled-and-brushed texture create the softly glowing dimensional finish on the bedroom wall shown below. The finish takes a little time to execute because the texture compound must have adequate time to dry before the base coat of color and glazing can be applied. Sweeping a wallpaper paste brush in arch-shape strokes over wet texture compound forms the subtle pattern. Pearlescent glaze medium mixed with paint produces an iridescent patina that enhances the textured pattern and creates shimmering highlights. The use of texture medium as a base for this technique makes it well suited for walls that have hard-to-conceal flaws.

INSTRUCTIONS

Mask ceiling, baseboards, and trim with painter's tape.

1 Use a large putty knife to apply Venetian plaster compound in a 3-foot-square section.

2 Use a wallpaper paste brush to sweep through the wet plaster compound, making overlapping arch-shape strokes. Moving to an adjacent area, continue to apply, then brush through the plaster compound until the entire wall is textured. Allow to dry completely.

3 Paint the entire wall in the periwinkle blue base-coat color. Paint two coats if necessary. Let dry overnight.

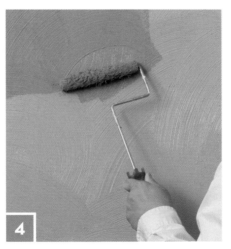

4 Using a plastic container with printed measurements, measure 4 parts iridescent pearl glaze medium to 1 part purple paint into a clean bucket. Mix enough glaze for the entire project so the intensity of the glaze color is consistent. The total amount of glaze mixture should equal the amount of base-coat color applied for one-coat coverage (see page 13). Fill a 3-gallon bucket half full of clean water for rinsing lint-free cloths. Starting at the top of the wall, use a trim brush to cut in the glaze mixture then use the mini roller to roll glaze onto a 4-foot-square section of wall.

5 Immediately wipe off the excess glaze using the dampened lint-free cotton cloth, allowing glaze to settle into the recessed areas. Use a clean area of the dampened cotton cloth to gently pat the wet glaze to blend and smooth it out. Turn to a clean area of the dampened cotton cloth and gently wipe off some of the highest spots to reveal highlights. Move to an adjacent area and repeat rolling on glaze and wiping it off until the entire wall is complete. Allow to dry.

Glaze Wash

Just as layering fabric patterns adds depth and variety to a room's color scheme, layering washes of colored glazes on a wall creates visual texture. This technique is easily accomplished by painters of all skill levels and requires only a few simple supplies. Apply as many layers as you like using subtle tint variations or bold contrasts. You can choose tones from the same color family or incorporate coordinating hues from your entire color scheme. For a subtle effect choose two hues from the same paint sample strip. To add a bit more interest use two paint hues in the same family but with different formulations such as the yellow-green paired with the blue-green shown opposite. For even more contrast layer on a third complementary color. The finished look will vary from room to room because each painter works in a unique way. This technique supports any decorating style from contemporary to casual.

SKILL LEVEL
Beginner

SPECIAL TOOLS
a. Glaze medium
b. Mini roller
c. Cheesecloth

a.

b.

c.

TOOLS
2-inch-wide low-tack painter's tape

Drop cloth

Stir sticks

Paint tray

Standard roller frame with 9-inch roller cover

2-inch tapered trim brush

2 plastic containers with printed measurements

Plastic 3-gallon bucket

Mini roller paint tray

PAINT
Semigloss latex for all colors

LIGHT GREEN FOR BASE COAT

YELLOW GREEN FOR GLAZE COAT

BLUE-GREEN FOR GLAZE COAT

TIP

Explore your color options by painting sample boards. Use darker shades over a light base coat. Or, for a dramatic result, use light hues over a medium- or dark-value base.

Glaze Techniques

Glaze Wash

INSTRUCTIONS

Mask ceiling, baseboards, and trim with painter's tape. Paint the entire wall in the light green base-coat color. Paint two coats if necessary. Leave tape on; let the paint dry overnight.

Use a plastic container with printed measurements to mix 4 parts glaze to 1 part medium green paint. In another container mix 4 parts glaze to 1 part medium blue-green paint. Mix enough glaze for the entire project so the intensities of the glaze colors are consistent. The glaze coverage on the wall on page 87 is about 50 percent yellow green mixture and 50 percent blue-green mixture.

Fill a 3-gallon bucket half full of clean water for rinsing the cheesecloth.

TIP

To keep the process flowing smoothly, work with a partner. One person rolls on the glaze mixture while the other blends the glaze with cheesecloth.

Use a trim brush to apply glaze along taped edges. This will ensure neat and consistent coverage.

Pour medium green glaze mixture into a mini roller paint tray. Lightly load a mini roller with the glaze mix. Using a light touch roll the glaze onto the wall, letting the roller skip over some areas. Complete an irregularly shaped area about 2×2 feet.

Working quickly while the glaze is still wet, dampen a piece of cheesecloth with water and wring it out thoroughly. Loosely bunch the cheesecloth and begin to dab and smudge the wet glaze mixture to remove some of the glaze and create a mottled appearance. Working one area at a time, finish glazing the wall. Let dry.

Repeat Step 1 using the medium blue-green glaze mixture. Use this glaze color sparingly so that the base-coat color and the first glaze mix color remain visible.

While the glaze mixture is still wet, pat and blend, making sure you leave areas where the base coat and lightest glaze color show through. As the cheesecloth becomes saturated with glaze, rinse and wring it out thoroughly before continuing to blend the glaze. Let dry.

Variation A

Medium blue and blue-green washed over light blue.

Variation B

Deep raspberry red washed over pink.

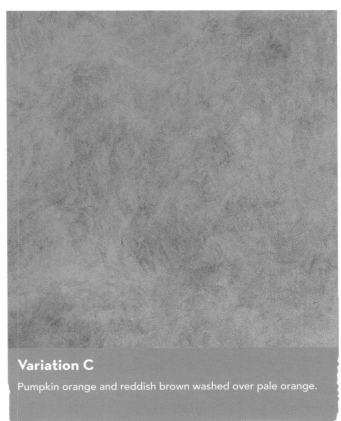

Variation C

Pumpkin orange and reddish brown washed over pale orange.

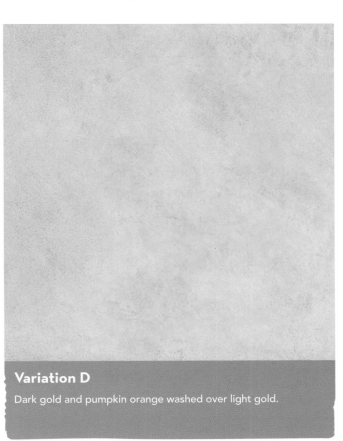

Variation D

Dark gold and pumpkin orange washed over light gold.

Creative Crinkle

Paint a bold textural look and color gradations on your walls using tinted glazes and plastic sheeting in this easy-to-apply finish. This dramatic technique involves a minimum of tools and expertise. Simply mix paint with glaze medium, apply it over a base coat with a roller, and then bunch and press a sheet of plastic to the wall to partially remove the mixture and create a crinkled pattern. Two tinted glaze mixtures are rolled over a warm-color base coat in this example. However additional glaze colors may be used to produce even more variation and interest. The lightest shades of mixed glaze are applied first, then the darkest tones are added. The weight of plastic used and how it is manipulated while removing the glaze mixture determine the pattern. This technique blends with any decorating style and looks great in any room.

SKILL LEVEL
Beginner

SPECIAL TOOLS
a. Glaze medium
b. 2 mini rollers
c. Plastic drop cloth

a.

b.

c.

TOOLS
2-inch-wide low-tack painter's tape

Drop cloth

Stir sticks

Paint tray

Standard roller frame with 9-inch roller cover

2-inch tapered trim brush

2 plastic containers with printed measurements

2 large plastic buckets for mixing glazes

Scissors

Lint-free cotton cloths

PAINT
Semigloss latex for all colors

PALE ORANGE FOR BASE COAT

MEDIUM ORANGE FOR GLAZE COAT

DARK ORANGE FOR SECOND GLAZE COAT

TIP

Use a base coat and glaze colors in the same color family for best results—for example a series of warm reds or cool blues. When picking colors choose base coat and glaze hues that are high contrast for a bold statement or low contrast for a soft look.

TIP

To keep the process flowing smoothly, work with a partner. One person rolls on the glaze mixtures while the other applies the plastic that removes the glazes.

If the completed texture is not satisfactory, wad up another piece of plastic wrap and add more crinkles. But be sure to do all of the crinkling while the glaze is still wet and workable.

Creative Crinkle

INSTRUCTIONS

Mask ceiling, baseboards, and trim with painter's tape. Paint the entire wall in the pale orange base-coat color. Paint two coats if necessary. Leave tape on; let dry overnight.

Using a plastic container with printed measurements, measure 4 parts glaze to 1 part medium orange paint into a clean bucket. In another bucket mix 4 parts glaze to 1 part dark orange paint. Mix enough glaze for the entire project so the intensities of the glaze colors are consistent. The total amount of glaze mixture should equal the amount of base-coat color applied for one-coat coverage (see page 13). The glaze coverage on this wall is about 80 percent medium orange mixture and 20 percent dark orange mixture.

Use scissors to cut manageable pieces of plastic approximately 2×3 feet.

TIP

Survey your work frequently while applying the glaze and crinkling to make any changes. It is not a good idea to add more glaze mixture or crinkle after the wall is dry. You may end up with a few inconsistencies as you work, but unique features add personality and a custom look to the wall.

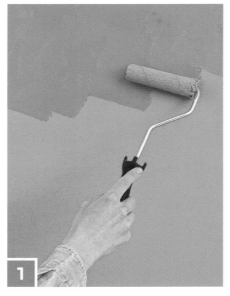

1

Use a trim brush to cut in the medium orange glaze mixture next to the ceiling. Then use the mini roller to roll glaze down from the top of the wall in sweeping strokes, filling in an irregularly shaped area about 4×4 feet.

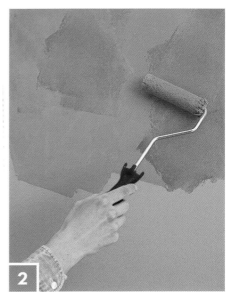

2

Immediately, using a second mini roller, randomly apply some of the dark orange glaze mixture over the medium orange glazed area.

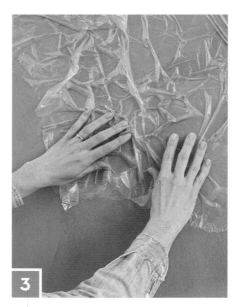

3

While the glaze is wet apply a piece of precut plastic to the wall. Arrange the plastic as desired, letting it form random wrinkles. Press it flat with the palms of your hands. Avoid dragging your fingers across the plastic because lines will appear.

4

Starting at an upper corner carefully peel the plastic off. Avoid dragging the plastic through the wet glaze so it won't smear your crinkle pattern.

5

Check for drips, then blot and blend any uneven areas with a piece of scrunched-up plastic. Quickly move to an adjacent area and repeat the glaze rolling and crinkling process. The plastic can be reused a few times. When it becomes saturated and no longer removes the paint-glaze mixture, discard it and use a clean piece of plastic. As you work the technique across the wall, overlap the previously crinkled areas, blending the paint-glaze mixture as you go. Finish one entire wall and let dry before moving to the adjacent wall. When painting the adjacent wall, immediately clean up any overlap in the corners with a damp cloth.

TIP

Paint one or more sample boards to explore color options. A light base color and progressively darker glaze top coats provide the most successful combination.

Adjust the look by experimenting with heavier- or lighter-weight plastic. A painter's plastic drop cloth, plastic dry-cleaning bags, or heavy garbage bags all give different results. Heavy plastic removes a lot of glaze and creates bolder wrinkles. Lightweight plastic removes little glaze and creates finer wrinkles.

Variation A

This sample was glazed over a light blue base coat using 50 percent purple-blue and 50 percent medium blue.

Variation B

This sample was glazed over a light yellow base coat using 100 percent medium yellow.

Variation C

This sample was glazed over a pale green base coat using 50 percent medium green, 25 percent olive green, and 25 percent dark green.

Variation D

This sample was glazed over a bright red base coat using 100 percent cranberry.

SKILL LEVEL

Beginner

SPECIAL TOOLS

a. Glaze medium

b. Chip brush

c. Large flat sponge

a.

b.

c.

TOOLS

2-inch-wide low-tack painter's tape

Drop cloth

Stir sticks

Paint tray

Standard roller frame with 9-inch roller cover

Mini roller with 4-inch roller cover

Plastic container with printed measurements

2 large plastic buckets

Lint-free cotton cloths

PAINT

Semigloss latex for base and glaze colors

WHITE LATEX STAIN-BLOCKING PRIMER

WHITE FOR BASE COAT

MEDIUM BLUE FOR GLAZE COAT

Pickling

Breathe new life into old, drab-looking wood paneling with a fresh coat of color. Pulling a damp flat sponge through a rolled-on coat of tinted glaze medium simulates the look of woodgrain. A coat of high-hiding white primer blocks out the dark paneling color, and a base coat of white semigloss paint yields a smooth surface so that the sponge glides easily when pulled through the glaze mixture. The sponge used—a tile grouting sponge available at home centers—has square edges and is made of dense foam without large pores. Midtone and pastel hues work best for this treatment.

INSTRUCTIONS

Mask ceiling, baseboards, and trim with painter's tape. Paint the entire wall in the white stain-blocking primer. Let dry. Paint the entire wall with the white base-coat color. Paint two coats if necessary. Leave tape on; let the primer dry overnight.

Using a plastic container with printed measurements, measure 4 parts glaze to 1 part medium blue paint into a clean bucket. Mix enough glaze for the entire project so the intensity of the glaze color is consistent. The total amount of glaze mixture should equal the amount of base-coat color applied for one-coat coverage.

Fill a large bucket half full of clean water for rinsing the sponge. Dampen a large, flat sponge and wring it out thoroughly.

Working on one paneling groove at a time use a chip brush to work glaze into the groove.

Working quickly, immediately use the damp sponge to wipe off the excess glaze mixture, allowing the glaze to stay only in the grooves. Continue to brush the glaze into the grooves and wipe off the excess until the entire wall is completed. Allow to dry.

Working on one paneling section at a time, use the mini roller to roll the glaze mixture between the grooves.

Immediately drag the sponge vertically through the glaze from ceiling to floor in one pass to create a streaked effect. Be sure to place the sponge so that it does not overlap the previous paneling section. If your ceilings are high, you will need to use a ladder to reach the ceiling and start pulling the sponge downward. Make a few dry runs to practice stepping down the ladder as you pull the sponge through the glaze.

Wipe off any excess glaze that may have smeared onto the neighboring unglazed section. Repeat rolling and wiping the glaze mixture until the wall is complete. Allow to dry.

Sponge Paint

Add visual depth and interest to plain walls with a quick and easy sponged-on coat of tinted glaze. A favorite among both beginning and experienced painters, sponge painting is a technique that anyone can master. It requires a minimum of steps to complete and only one specialty painting tool—a large natural sponge. Endless possible color combinations, the unique shape of each sponge, and the individuality of each painter's touch mean no two rooms will look the same. Whether you sponge on a heavy application of high-contrast color or dab on delicate tone-on-tone hues, the technique yields dramatic results. And you can expand beyond one tinted glaze color. You can create even more interesting color variations by applying additional tints over the basic glaze, either while it is still wet or after it has dried. This simple paint treatment brings endless possibilities to any decorating style.

SKILL LEVEL

Beginner

SPECIAL TOOLS

a. Paper plates

b. Natural sponges

c. Sponge roller

d. Glaze medium

a.

b.

c.

d.

TOOLS

2-inch-wide low-tack painter's tape

Drop cloth

Stir sticks

Paint tray

Standard roller frame with 9-inch roller cover

2-inch tapered trim brush

Plastic container with printed measurements

2 large plastic buckets

Paper towels

Cardboard

PAINT

Semigloss latex for both colors

MEDIUM ORANGE FOR BASE COAT

DARK REDDISH BROWN FOR GLAZE COAT

TIP

Explore your color options by painting sample boards. Try reversing base-coat and top-coat colors for a dramatic difference in the final result.

To keep the process flowing smoothly, work with a partner. One person sponges on the glaze mixture while the other removes and blends the glaze.

Use a trim brush or sponge roller to apply glaze along taped edges. This will ensure neat and consistent coverage.

Glaze Techniques

Sponge Paint

INSTRUCTIONS

Mask ceiling, baseboards, and trim with painter's tape. Paint the entire wall in the medium orange base-coat color. Paint two coats if necessary. Leave tape on; let the paint dry overnight.

Use a plastic container with printed measurements to measure 4 parts glaze to 1 part dark reddish brown paint into a clean bucket. Mix enough glaze for the entire project so the intensity of the glaze color is consistent. The total amount of glaze mixture should equal the amount of base-coat color applied for one-coat coverage (see page 13).

1 Pour a small amount of the dark reddish brown glaze mixture onto a paper plate.

2 Dampen a sponge with water and wring it out thoroughly. Dip the sponge into the glaze mixture and blot the excess onto a pad of absorbent paper towels. On a piece of cardboard, dab the sponge lightly, overlapping the edges of color and rotating the sponge, creating a random effect. When you're comfortable with the color intensity and sponge pattern, start in an upper corner and apply the glaze to the wall.

3 Work over one 4×4-foot irregularly shaped area at a time, dipping the sponge into the glaze mixture as needed.

4 When the sponge becomes saturated with the glaze mixture, rinse it in a bucket of water and wring it out thoroughly before continuing.

5 After sponging the 4-foot-square area, dampen a clean sponge in clean water and wring it out thoroughly. Using the damp sponge dab the wet glaze mixture to remove some of it so the base-coat color peeks through. Blend any uneven areas. Rinse and wring the sponge as needed. Move to an adjacent area and continue the process, following Steps 3-5 until the entire wall is finished. Let the paint dry.

Variation A

Medium blue sponge painted over light blue.

Variation B

Pumpkin orange sponge painted over golden yellow.

Variation C

Deep raspberry red sponge painted over bright red.

Variation D

Leaf green sponge painted over light green.

SKILL LEVEL

Beginner

SPECIAL TOOLS

a. Glaze medium

b. Feather duster

a.

b.

TOOLS

2-inch-wide low-tack painter's tape

Drop cloth

Stir sticks

Paint tray

Standard roller frame with 9-inch roller cover

2-inch tapered trim brush

2 plastic containers with printed measurements

Paper towels

Scrap piece of cardboard

PAINT

Semigloss latex for all colors

PALE GOLDEN YELLOW FOR BASE COAT

IVORY FOR GLAZE COAT

MEDIUM RUSTY RED FOR GLAZE COAT

Feather Duster

If you like the look of handmade paper with its nubby texture and flecks of color, you can impart that same look to your walls. This quick-and-easy technique requires only one special tool—a household feather duster. When dipped into a paint-and-glaze mixture and lightly dabbed onto a base-coat wall, it makes a pattern that closely resembles the inclusions in handmade paper. If you "dust" on one glaze color in a tone one or two shades lighter or darker than your base-coat color, the result will be a subtle pattern of colored flecks. Add a contrasting glaze color and the effect will be more dramatic, as in the example below.

INSTRUCTIONS

Mask ceiling, baseboards, and trim with painter's tape. Paint the entire wall in the pale golden yellow base-coat color. Paint two coats if necessary. Leave tape on; let the paint dry overnight.

Use a plastic container with printed measurements to mix 4 parts glaze to 1 part ivory paint. In another container mix 4 parts glaze to 1 part medium rusty red paint. Mix enough glaze for the entire project so the intensities of the glaze colors are consistent (see page 13).

Pour ivory glaze mixture into a paint tray. Dab the tips of the feather duster into the puddle of glaze. Tap the loaded feather duster on the inclined area of the paint tray to evenly distribute the glaze throughout the feather tips. Test the glaze distribution and pattern by tapping the glaze-loaded feather duster on a piece of scrap cardboard. When you are satisfied with the pattern, start tapping the glaze onto the base-coat wall. Rotate the feather duster as you apply the glaze to create a random pattern. Complete the entire wall. Let dry.

Repeat Step 1 using the rusty red glaze mixture. Use this glaze color sparingly so that the base-coat color and the first glaze mix color remain visible. Let dry.

After completing the entire wall, stand back and evaluate the results. Make adjustments as necessary.

Glazed Wallpaper

Walls clad with paintable embossed wallpaper give the decorative painter a new dimension in possibilities. And antiquing the textured surface with a wash of tinted glaze medium enhances the wallpaper's design elements. The process is simple enough for a novice painter to accomplish and requires few supplies. Paintable wallpaper, as its name implies, is specially made to be painted. Base-coating the wallpaper after it is applied to the wall is the key to success. This step not only gives the wall a coat of overall color, but it also seals the paper so that the glaze top coat will not soak in and create blotches. Whether your project calls for whimsical, formal, or modern, there are dozens of paintable wallpaper designs available at decorating centers and online that will fit any decorating style.

SKILL LEVEL

Beginner

SPECIAL TOOLS

a. Embossed
   wallpaper

b. Glaze medium

c. Lint-free
   cotton cloths

a.

b.

c.

TOOLS

2-inch-wide
low-tack
painter's tape

Drop cloth

Stir sticks

Paint tray

Standard roller
frame with 9-inch
roller cover

2-inch tapered
trim brush

Plastic container
with printed
measurements

2 large plastic
buckets

Mini roller
with 4-inch
roller cover

PAINT

Semigloss latex for both colors

OFF-WHITE FOR BASE COAT

MEDIUM GOLD FOR GLAZE COAT

INSTRUCTIONS

Hang the wallpaper following the manufacturer's directions. Mask ceiling, baseboards, and trim with painter's tape. To seal the wallpaper and prevent the glaze from soaking into the paper, paint the entire wall in the off-white base-coat color. Paint two coats if necessary. Leave tape on; let the paint dry overnight.

Use a plastic container with printed measurements to measure 4 parts glaze to 1 part medium gold paint into a clean bucket. Mix enough glaze for the entire project so the intensity of the glaze color is consistent. The total amount of glaze mixture should equal the amount of base-coat color applied for one-coat coverage (see page 13).

Fill another bucket half full of clean water for rinsing cloths. Dampen a cloth and wring it out.

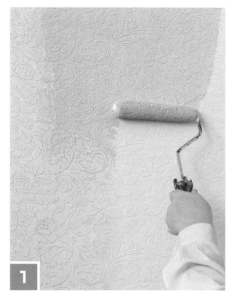

1 Cut in the medium gold glaze mixture along the ceiling with a trim brush. Then using the mini roller, roll the glaze mixture down from the top of the wall to fill in an area about 4×4 feet.

2 Immediately wipe off the excess glaze using the dampened lint-free cotton cloth, allowing the glaze to settle into the recessed areas of the wallpaper.

3 Use a clean area of the dampened cotton cloth to gently pat the wet glaze to blend and smooth out the glaze.

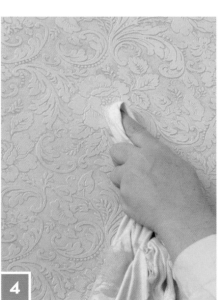

4 Turn to a clean area of the dampened cotton cloth and gently wipe off some of the highest spots on the embossed wallpaper to reveal highlights.

5 Repeat Steps 1–4 until the entire wall is complete. Allow to dry.

Handpainted Vertical Stripes

In a subtle tone-on-tone color scheme or in fun-loving and circus-bright colors, stripes easily add interest to plain walls. The casual charm of this treatment is enhanced by the slight imperfections that the handpainting produces. The light blue base coat in the space shown below provides the background, and handpainted stripes of pale green complete the pattern. The soft shades of green and blue are close in value, making paint coverage easy. With a bit of practice and the proper brush, handpainted stripes are simple to paint. When planning your room's layout a good rule to follow to create a pleasing overall stripe pattern is to use 4- to 7-inch-wide stripes. Handpainted stripes work well for casual spaces as well as for children's rooms.

SKILL LEVEL

Intermediate

SPECIAL TOOLS

a. Level with printed ruler

b. 2-inch tapered trim brush

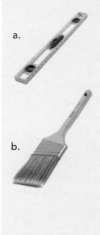

a.

b.

TOOLS

Drop cloth

Stir sticks

Paint tray

Standard roller frame with 9-inch roller cover

Tape measure

Colored pencil

PAINT

Semigloss latex for both colors

LIGHT BLUE FOR BASE COAT

LIGHT GREEN FOR STRIPES

INSTRUCTIONS

Mask ceiling, baseboards, and trim with painter's tape. Paint the entire wall in the light blue base-coat color. Paint two coats if necessary. Leave tape on; let the paint dry overnight.

To divide the room into stripes of equal width, first measure the total width of each wall in inches. Next divide the total wall width by the desired stripe width to determine the number of stripes. The stripes shown here measure 5 inches, but you may choose another stripe width for your walls to get the look you desire. You can have stripes end in corners or wrap around corners and continue on the adjacent wall. Wrapping stripes around corners looks better on walls that aren't square.

1 To lay out the stripes, use a tape measure and colored pencil to measure and mark all the walls with an upper and lower mark for each stripe. Then use a long level to draw in vertical lines from ceiling to baseboard, connecting upper and lower marks at each stripe interval. The level will ensure that the lines stay vertical and parallel to one another. Periodically check the stripes to make sure they remain parallel and even.

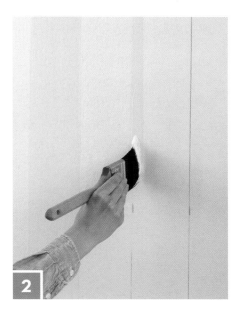

2 Working one stripe at a time, cut in along the ceiling with a trim brush and light green paint. Then paint the left edge of the stripe, covering the pencil line. Reload the paintbrush as needed so the color is opaque and even.

3 Fill in the center of the stripe using long vertical strokes.

4 Cut in the right edge of the stripe, covering the pencil line. Cut in along the baseboard. Repeat for each remaining stripe. Touch up any uneven spots.

Variation

This dining room boasts handpainted stripes above a chair rail that are rendered in a color scheme of light, medium, and dark blue. Wide medium blue stripes were first painted over a light blue base coat. Then each medium blue stripe was punctuated with a dark blue pinstripe on each edge for a tailored yet casual look.

Taped Vertical Stripes

Crisp-edge painted stripes give a tailored finish to any room and complement any decorating style. This basic paint treatment is easy to accomplish. The secret to stripes with clean, straight edges is to seal the edge of the low-tack painter's tape with the base coat color before rolling on the stripe color. Stripes can be painted in an endless variety of widths and colors. Fabrics are a great source of ideas for color combinations and stripe patterns. Combining different paint sheens provides even more possibilities; for example, if the base coat is flat, stripes painted in semigloss yield visual texture as well as pattern. When planning your project consider the room's dimensions. Wide stripes make small rooms seem larger while narrow stripes lead the eye upward and appear to raise the ceiling height. It is a good idea to paint one or more sample boards to explore color options and adjust contrast and stripe width if necessary.

SKILL LEVEL

Beginner

SPECIAL TOOLS

a. Tape measure

b. Level with printed ruler

c. Low-tack painter's tape

d. Mini roller

a.

b.

c.

d.

TOOLS

Drop cloth

Stir sticks

Paint tray

Standard roller frame with 9-inch roller cover

Colored pencil

Chip brush

PAINT

Semigloss latex for both colors

LIGHT BLUE FOR BASE COAT

SLIGHTLY DARKER BLUE FOR STRIPES

Stripes & Blocks

Taped Vertical Stripes

INSTRUCTIONS

Mask ceiling, baseboards, and trim with painter's tape. Paint the entire wall in the light blue base-coat color. Paint two coats if necessary. Leave tape on; let the paint dry overnight.

To divide the room into stripes of equal width, first measure the total width of each wall in inches. Next divide the total wall width by the desired stripe width to determine the number of stripes. The stripes shown here measure 5 inches, but you may choose a different stripe width for your walls. You can plan your layout to have stripes end in corners or wrap around corners and continue on the adjacent wall. Wrapping stripes around corners looks better on walls that aren't square.

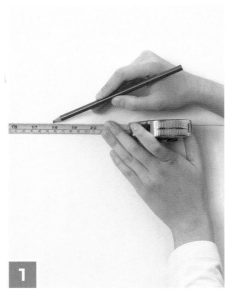

1

To lay out the stripes, use a tape measure and colored pencil to measure and mark all the walls with an upper and lower mark for each stripe.

2

Then use a long level to draw in vertical lines from ceiling to baseboard, connecting upper and lower marks at each stripe interval. The level will ensure that the lines stay vertical and parallel to one another. Periodically check the stripes to make sure they remain parallel and even.

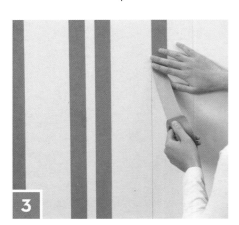

3

Apply low-tack painter's tape along the outside edges of each alternating stripe, pressing down firmly on the inner edges of the tape.

4

Use the chip brush to repaint the base coat color along the taped edges of each stripe. This seals the tape to the wall and helps prevent the top coat of paint from bleeding underneath. Allow to dry.

5

Use the mini roller to paint the stripes. Paint two coats if necessary to ensure solid coverage, letting the paint dry between coats.

6

After the paint has set up slightly and begins to dry it loses its shiny, wet look. This is the time to carefully remove the tape by pulling outward from the wall at a 90-degree angle. Allow paint to dry.

Variation A

Stripes in muted shades of yellow, blue, and green lend a modern touch to this living room. No tape is needed for this striped pattern. Measure and mark the stripes, then roll on alternating yellow and blue paint. Strips of green-painted 1¾-inch-wide molding cover the area where the painted stripes join.

Variation B

Wide stripes painted in a subtle color scheme of green and blue create a serene backdrop for this casual living space. The key to creating this look is using the same tone for the two stripe colors. To duplicate this look choose two colors that are on the same position on a paint sample strip.

Variation C

The stripes in this bedroom were extended to cover the ceiling in a squared-off pattern that creates a canopy of color. The bright yellow hue lends a lively pop of color to the balance of the neutral scheme.

Variation D

Crisp bright green stripes painted on a white base-coat wall in this teen's room create a lively background for the punchy color scheme. The green stripes are a perfect choice to make the bright orange and pink elements stand out. The white stripes, flooring, and accessories add a neutral note to the mix.

Variation E

This room's window treatments inspired the color scheme and pinstripe pattern on the walls. Wide blue stripes are painted on a white base coat, and then narrow stripes are taped off and painted last.

Taped Horizontal Stripes

Contemporary and adventurous, horizontal stripes make a bold statement in any room. Painting stripes one or two tones darker than the base coat in the living room, shown opposite, takes this basic beige wall from boring to dynamic. Unlike vertical stripes, which lead the eye up and create the illusion of vertical space, horizontal stripes lead the eye along the wall and appear to expand the space outward. Paint only one wall for a focal point in the room or wrap stripes around corners to include two or more walls. When designing your stripe width and color arrangement, sketch your ideas on graph paper to help visualize your plan. For an overall pattern of horizontal stripes, widths from 14 to 20 inches give the most pleasing effect. Use varying stripe widths to create borders, simulate architectural elements or create a more intricate pattern on a focal-point wall.

SKILL LEVEL

Beginner

SPECIAL TOOLS

a. Tape measure

b. Level with printed ruler

c. Low-tack painter's tape

d. Mini roller

a.

b.

c.

d.

TOOLS

Drop cloth

Stir sticks

Paint tray

Standard roller frame with 9-inch roller cover

Graph paper

Colored pencil

Chip brush

PAINT

Semigloss latex for both colors

LIGHT BEIGE BASE COAT

SLIGHTLY DARKER BEIGE FOR STRIPES

Stripes & Blocks

Taped Horizontal Stripes

INSTRUCTIONS

Mask ceiling, baseboards, and trim with painter's tape. Paint the entire wall in the light beige base-coat color. Paint two coats if necessary. Leave tape on; let the paint dry overnight.

To divide the room into stripes of equal width, first measure the height of each wall in inches. Next divide the total wall height by the desired stripe width to determine the number of stripes. The stripes shown here measure 16 inches wide, but you may choose a different stripe width for your walls to get the look you desire.

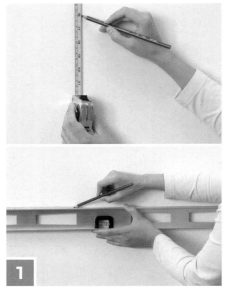

Starting at the ceiling use a tape measure and colored pencil to make a series of measurement marks moving vertically down the wall.

Use a long level to draw horizontal lines, connecting the marks at each stripe interval. The level will ensure that the lines stay horizontal and parallel to one another. Periodically check the stripes to make sure they remain parallel and even.

Apply low-tack painter's tape along the outside edges of each alternating stripe, pressing down firmly on the inner edges of the tape.

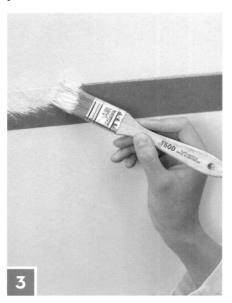

Use the chip brush to repaint the base coat color along the taped edges of each stripe. This seals the tape to the wall and helps prevent the top coat of paint from bleeding underneath. Allow to dry.

Use the mini roller to paint the stripes. Paint two coats if necessary to ensure solid coverage, letting the paint dry between coats.

After the paint has set up slightly and begins to dry it loses its shiny, wet look. This is the time to carefully remove the tape by pulling outward from the wall at a 90-degree angle. Allow paint to dry.

Variation A

In this dining room stripes of varying widths were designed to mimic architectural elements. The stripe arrangement on the upper wall implies crown molding while the lower stripes stop at chair rail height, creating a wainscot effect.

Variation B

Two wide horizontal stripes in tones of the same green simply but effectively to accentuate the boxy style of this room's design elements. The pattern was planned so the stripes are in line with the window muntins, creating a smooth line that flows uninterrupted around the room.

Variation C

Stripes of varying widths rendered in bold hues create an eye-popping backdrop for the display shelves and oversize headboard in this teen's room. The floating shelves are placed on the wall so that they seem to be an extension of the painted stripes.

Variation D

Carefully coordinating the color scheme and design elements is the key to this room's success. The bold-hue stripes are matched by a large-scale pattern on the pillow. Solid neutrals on furniture and floor covering provide a resting place for the eye.

Variation E

Two tones of perky pink surround the walls in this girl's room to accentuate the bold graphics on the fabrics and accessories. White furniture, woodwork, and flooring lend visual balance and keep the stripes from overpowering the other design elements.

Variation F

A wide blue stripe bordered with narrower off-white stripes divides the wall in this teen room and plays off the patterns on the bed's comforter and pillow shams. The remainder of the wall above the upper white stripe is painted a solid beige; below the lower white stripe, dark brown completes the color scheme.

Block Border

Painting a border of layered blocks is a simple but effective way to tie a room's color scheme together and add a graphic decorative element at the same time. A border of blocks yields a big impact in a small space. The border in the kitchen below creates a decorative backsplash, but the same pattern would be effective painted around an entire room at either chair rail or ceiling height. Bold colors are perfect for a contemporary look while tone-on-tone hues convey a softer, more subtle statement.

SKILL LEVEL

Beginner

SPECIAL TOOLS

a. Level with printed ruler

b. Low-tack painter's tape

c. Mini roller

a.

b.

c.

TOOLS

Drop cloth

Stir sticks

Paint tray

Standard roller frame with 9-inch roller cover

Graph paper

Tape measure

Colored pencil

Chip brush

PAINT

Satin latex for all colors

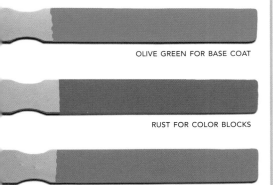

OLIVE GREEN FOR BASE COAT

RUST FOR COLOR BLOCKS

PURPLE FOR COLOR BLOCKS

INSTRUCTIONS

Mask ceiling, baseboards, and trim with painter's tape. Paint the entire wall in the olive green base-coat color. Paint two coats if necessary. Leave tape on; let the paint dry overnight.

The block border shown is located between the countertop and upper cabinet in a kitchen. To lay out the block border, measure the length and height of the area to be painted. Draw a sketch on graph paper to help you visualize block sizes and color placement. The blocks shown are 18 inches square. If you are painting a block pattern on more than one wall, continue the blocks around the corners.

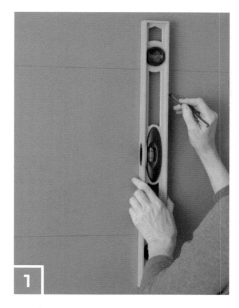

Use the tape measure and colored pencil to mark upper and lower lines for each block interval along the entire border. Use the level and colored pencil to draw lines connecting upper and lower marks at each block interval. The level will ensure that the lines stay vertical and parallel to one another. Because alternating blocks are painted first and allowed to dry before adjacent blocks are painted, tape off alternating blocks with low-tack painter's tape.

Repaint the olive green base-coat color along the taped edges of the blocks. This seals the tape to the wall and helps prevent the paint from bleeding underneath. Allow to dry. Use the mini roller to paint alternating blocks with rust. Paint two coats if necessary, letting the paint dry between coats. After the paint has set up and loses its wet look, remove the tape by pulling outward from the wall at a 90-degree angle. Allow paint to dry.

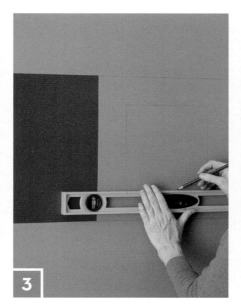

Use the level and colored pencil to measure and mark the inner blocks along the entire border.

Use low-tack painter's tape to tape off all inner blocks along the entire border.

After using the chip brush to repaint the appropriate base-coat color along the taped edges of each inner block, use the mini roller to paint all inner blocks with purple. Remove the tape and allow the paint to dry.

Intersecting Blocks

You can create an artistic statement in a contemporary space without expensive artwork or a lot of time. Simply painting a couple of large-scale intersecting color blocks punctuated with rows of smaller blocks quickly delivers a graphic punch to a plain wall. Choosing a group of colors is easy. Simply pick four hues from the same paint sample card. Use the darkest for the base-coat color on the entire wall and then layer on two large overlapping rectangles in the next two lighter hues. Finally use the lightest color to add rows of smaller rectangles. To assist in designing a pleasing composition, use low-tack painter's tape to lay out the large rectangles on your wall. Then stand back and evaluate size and proportion and make adjustments until you're pleased with the results. Draw a sketch of the layout on graph paper and note the final measurements. Minimal furnishings of clean-line design accentuate the contemporary look of this paint treatment.

SKILL LEVEL

Beginner

SPECIAL TOOLS

a. Tape measure

b. Level with printed ruler

c. Mini roller

d. Torpedo level

a.

b.

c.

d.

TOOLS

Drop cloth

Stir sticks

Paint tray

Standard roller frame with 9-inch roller cover

Graph paper

2-inch-wide low-tack painter's tape

Colored pencil

Chip brush

PAINT

Satin latex for all colors

MEDIUM GREEN FOR BASE COAT

LIGHT GREEN FOR COLOR BLOCKS

LIGHTER GREEN FOR COLOR BLOCKS

LIGHTEST GREEN FOR COLOR BLOCKS

INSTRUCTIONS

Mask ceiling, baseboards, and trim with painter's tape. Paint the entire wall in the medium green base-coat color. Paint two coats if necessary. Leave tape on; let the paint dry overnight.

To lay out the wall with intersecting blocks, first measure the total height and width of the wall in inches. Draw a sketch on graph paper to help you visualize block sizes and color placement.

To lay out the large horizontal block, use the tape measure and colored pencil to measure and mark the wall for all four lines around the perimeter.

Use the long level and colored pencil to draw all four lines. The level will ensure that all lines stay square to one another.

Tape off the large horizontal block with the low-tack painter's tape. Use the chip brush to repaint the base coat color along the taped edges of the block. This seals the tape to the wall and helps prevent the top coat of paint from bleeding underneath. Allow to dry.

Use the mini roller to paint the block light green. Paint two coats if necessary, letting the paint dry between coats. After the paint has set up slightly and begins to dry it loses its shiny, wet look. This is the time to carefully remove the tape by pulling outward from the wall at a 90-degree angle. Allow paint to dry.

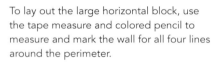

Repeat Steps 1-3 for the large vertical block, using the horizontal block color to seal the edges of the tape before rolling on the lighter green vertical block color. Remove the tape and allow the paint to dry. Use the tape measure and colored pencil to mark measurements for the two rows of small blocks. Use the torpedo level to mark the lines for each small block.

Use the chip brush to repaint the taped edges of each small block with the large vertical block color. Allow to dry. Use the mini roller to paint each small block with lightest green. Remove the tape and allow the paint to dry.

Allover Blocks

Painting a wall with blocks of solid color in either bold or subtle hues is an easy way to pack a lot of visual punch into a space. Whether you decide to paint one wall for a focal point or wrap the entire room in color blocks, planning is the key to success. Start by sketching a scaled drawing of your wall layout on graph paper. Visit your paint dealer to collect an assortment of paint sample strips, then cut them into square chips that fit your sketched grid. Place the chips on the grid and move them around until you are satisfied with the result.

The block size and color scheme you use depends on the effect you want to achieve. A large block pattern takes less time to paint than a small one. Paint bright-color blocks in rooms where you want to exude energy and stimulate the senses. For a serene or sophisticated statement, choose pastels in the same color family.

SKILL LEVEL

Beginner

SPECIAL TOOLS

a. Tape measure

b. Level with printed ruler

c. Low-tack painter's tape

d. Mini roller

a.

b.

c.

d.

TOOLS

Drop cloth

Stir sticks

Paint tray

Standard roller frame with 9-inch roller cover

Graph paper

Colored pencil

Chip brush

PAINT

Use any sheen latex desired for all colors

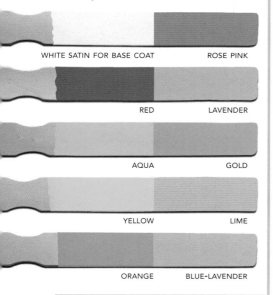

WHITE SATIN FOR BASE COAT   ROSE PINK

RED   LAVENDER

AQUA   GOLD

YELLOW   LIME

ORANGE   BLUE-LAVENDER

Allover Blocks

INSTRUCTIONS

Mask ceiling, baseboards, and trim with painter's tape. Paint the entire wall in the white base-coat color. Paint two coats if necessary. Leave tape on; let the paint dry overnight.

To divide the room into blocks, first measure the total height and width of each wall in inches. Draw a sketch on graph paper to help you visualize block sizes and color placement. The blocks shown on pages 118 and 119 are 24 inches square. If you are painting a block pattern on all walls, continue the blocks around corners. You can make slight adjustments to the block widths on adjacent walls if necessary but keep the height of the blocks the same on every wall so the block heights match up around the room.

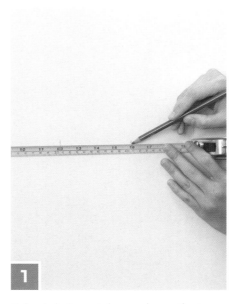

1

To begin laying out the panels, use the tape measure and colored pencil to measure and mark all the walls with an upper and lower mark for each vertical line.

2

Use the long level and colored pencil to draw in vertical lines to connect the upper and lower marks at each block interval. The level will ensure that the lines stay vertical and parallel to one another.

3

Use the tape measure and colored pencil to measure and mark all the walls at intervals for the horizontal lines.

4

Use the long level and colored pencil to draw in horizontal lines to complete the block pattern.

5

Because alternating blocks are painted first and allowed to dry before adjacent blocks are painted, tape off alternating blocks with the low-tack painter's tape.

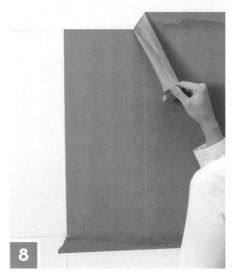

6 Use the chip brush to repaint the base-coat color along the taped edges of the block. This seals the tape to the wall and helps prevent the top coat of paint from bleeding underneath. Allow to dry.

7 Use the mini roller to paint the block. Paint two coats if necessary, letting the paint dry between coats.

8 After the paint has set up slightly and begins to dry it loses its shiny, wet look. This is the time to carefully remove the tape by pulling outward from the wall. Allow paint to dry.

9 Repeat the taping and painting process on adjacent blocks until the entire grid of blocks is complete. Remove all tape; allow to dry.

Variation

Brightly colored blocks of varying shapes and sizes float on the wall in this little girl's room. All of the blocks in this configuration can be painted at the same time since they don't abut one another. Before painting work out a plan on graph paper and experiment with color placement by filling in the plotted blocks with colored pencils. Keep furniture, window, and door placements in mind as you work out your overall design.

Vintage Damask

The damask pattern in the kitchen/dining area, opposite, stenciled in a deep gold hue over a tan base-coat color, creates a vintage wallpaper look. A light wash of brown glaze accentuates the aged appearance. Damask-pattern wallpaper stencils come in a wide variety of designs and are available online and at crafts retailers. These large-size stencils make the job of stenciling an entire room quick and easy. They come with registration marks so lining up repeats is simple once a level line is marked on the wall for a starting point. Using a foam stencil roller for stenciling allows you to cover large areas quickly. Varying the amount of pressure you apply while rolling the paint into the stencil openings creates areas of lighter and heavier coverage so the pattern appears faded and worn. Whether your style is traditional, vintage, or modern, oversize damask patterns work for nearly every decor.

SKILL LEVEL

Intermediate

SPECIAL TOOLS

a. Stencil adhesive

b. Stencil roller

c. Glaze medium

d. Lint-free cotton cloths

a.

b.

c.

d.

TOOLS

Drop cloth

Stir sticks

Paint tray

Standard roller frame with 9-inch roller cover

2-inch tapered trim brush

2-inch-wide low-tack painter's tape

Level with printed ruler

Colored chalk

Stencil, see Resources, page 190

Mini roller paint tray

Paper towels

Plastic container with printed measurements

PAINT

Semigloss latex for all colors

TAN FOR BASE COAT

DEEP GOLD FOR STENCILING

DARK BROWN FOR GLAZE COAT

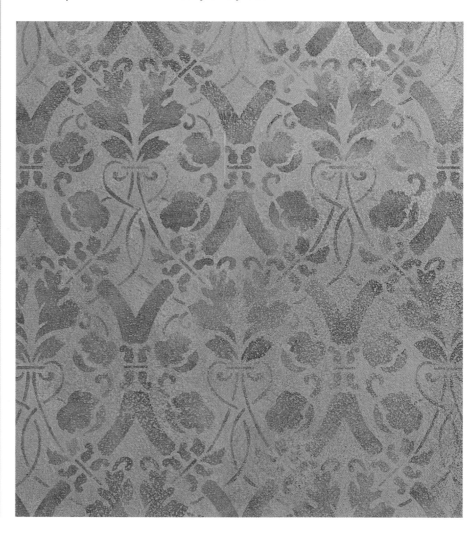

Stencil & Stamp

Vintage Damask

INSTRUCTIONS

Mask ceiling, baseboards, and trim with painter's tape. Paint the entire wall in the tan base-coat color. Paint two coats if necessary. Leave tape on; let the paint dry overnight.

TIP

When stenciling use as little paint as possible to prevent the paint from bleeding under the stencil.

1

The stencil motifs will interconnect, so the first stenciled motif must be level and plumb. To determine a starting point for the first stencil placement, measure and mark the center of one wall. Using a level and chalk, draw a center plumb line from ceiling to floor. Next draw a level line in chalk about head high, horizontally across the walls to be stenciled.

2

Spray the back of the stencil with the stencil adhesive. Apply the stencil to the wall, lining up the registration marks to the horizontal chalk line. Gently pat and smooth the stencil in place to ensure that all areas have adhered well. Mark a chalk dot in the top of each triangular registration mark.

Pour a small amount of deep gold paint into the mini roller tray. Saturate the stencil roller and roll off the excess paint onto a stack of absorbent paper towels. Too much paint on the roller can cause the paint to bleed under the stencil. Using light pressure on the stencil roller, apply the paint to the stencil. Check to make sure all stencil openings have been covered and fill in where necessary. Remove the stencil and let the paint dry.

3

Move the stencil to the repeat position by lining up two triangles with the dots you made. Position the stencil, mark the two opposite triangles, and continue to apply paint. Apply the first row of stencils horizontally across the entire wall.

4

Spray the back side of the stencil periodically as needed. You should be able to use the stencil five or six times before it is necessary to reapply adhesive.

After the first row is completed, return to the center and use the registration marks to align the next row under the first one.

5

Stencil the rows below all the way to the baseboard and above all the way to the ceiling. Let dry.

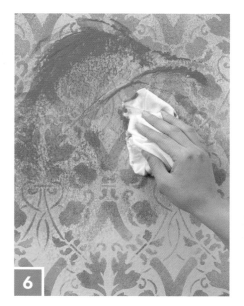

6

Using a plastic container with printed measurements, measure and mix 4 parts glaze to 1 part dark brown paint. Bunch a damp piece of soft, lint-free cloth and dip it into the glaze mixture. Wash the glaze onto the wall using a circular motion to create a softly stained effect. Use a trim brush for corners and around the molding, then go over the surface with the cloth to remove brushstrokes. Let dry.

TIP

Be careful to line up the stencil with the registration marks. This will keep the design running level and plumb. Very slight variations are acceptable but try to be as accurate as possible.

When stenciling tight areas and corners where bending the stencil is necessary, handle the stencil gently and avoid creasing it. Save these areas for last if possible.

Variation A

This wall illustrates another way to give a vintage look to stenciled damask. The wall is first base-coated with a pale rose hue, and then the damask stencil is applied with white. After the motifs have dried they are then randomly sanded with fine-grit sandpaper. A final top coat of very thin white glaze applied over the entire wall creates an aged look.

Variation B

This dining room features an antique lace effect that is easily accomplished using a damask stencil. The damask stencil is applied over a soft mauve base coat. The stenciling starts above the chair rail and stops level with the top of the window's woodwork. Instead of completing the entire upper motif, the stenciled design ends midway to create a curved border.

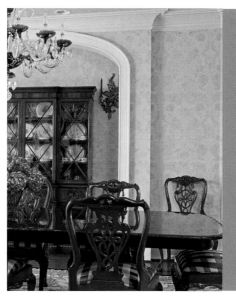

Variation C

The softly faded damask stencil in this dining room looks complicated but is easy to execute using a combination of techniques. The walls are first stenciled with soft hues, filling in the scrolls with gray and the flowers with mauve, and overlapping the colors when transitioning from one color to the next. After the paint has dried a light sanding with fine-grit sandpaper removes some of the paint to create a faded effect. Finally a pale gray glaze is brushed through from ceiling to floor using a wallpaper brush. The strié technique simulates antique silk damask.

SKILL LEVEL

Beginner

SPECIAL TOOLS

a. Stencil adhesive

b. Stencil roller

a.

b.

TOOLS

2-inch-wide low-tack painter's tape

Drop cloth

Stir sticks

Paint tray

Standard roller frame with 9-inch roller cover

2-inch tapered trim brush

Stencil, see Resources, page 190

Mini roller paint tray

Paper towels

PAINT

Semigloss latex for both colors

TURQUOISE FOR BASE COAT

PALE GREEN FOR STENCILING

Allover Paisley

A bright, fresh color scheme and an oversize paisley-motif stencil give the wall in the trendy bedroom below its graphic pop. Though the pattern looks as though the stencil repeats are placed at random, a careful examination reveals that they are actually plotted in groups of four, arranged in a pattern of diagonal rows. Careful planning and measuring are the keys to success. If you are planning to stencil two walls in a room and you need to wrap motifs around corners, save these repeats for last and press the stencil carefully into corners to minimize creasing its plastic. A bold pattern such as this paisley motif is best used on one or two accent walls.

INSTRUCTIONS

Mask ceiling, baseboards, and trim with painter's tape. Paint the entire wall in the turquoise base-coat color. Paint two coats if necessary. Leave tape on; let the paint dry overnight.

To plan the layout first make four photocopies of the stencil motif. Tape the paper copies onto the wall, experimenting with angles and distances from one another. When you are satisfied with the placements, measure the overall grouping dimensions. Then measure and mark the wall with small dots to indicate the center of each grouping. Start the first diagonal row in the upper left-hand corner of the wall.

Spray the back of the first stencil overlay with the stencil adhesive.

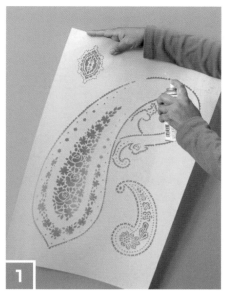

Apply the first overlay to the wall, adhesive side down, gently patting and smoothing to ensure that all areas have adhered well.

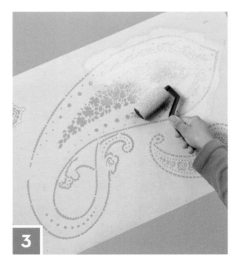

Pour a small amount of pale green paint into the mini roller tray. Saturate the stencil roller and roll off the excess paint onto a stack of absorbent paper towels. Too much paint on the roller can cause the paint to bleed under the stencil. Using light pressure on the stencil roller, apply the paint onto the stencil. Check to make sure all stencil openings have been covered and fill in where necessary. Remove the stencil and let the paint dry.

Spray the backside of the second overlay. Line up the registration marks of the second overlay and press into place.

Repeat Step 3 to stencil the second overlay. Let dry. Continue by placing the first overlay in the next position and repeating Steps 2–4. You should respray with adhesive after every 5 to 10 uses.

Raised-Texture Stencil

A gentle drift of applied dimensional leaves with a top coat of autumn-tone glazes creates the stunning focal point wall, opposite. A couple of key painting supplies make this technique easy to execute. Tinted Venetian plaster compound troweled into the openings of a stencil cut from extra thick plastic is the secret to success. On this wall the plaster compound is tinted the same color as the wall's base coat to save a step in the process. Special texturing stencils, available at crafts retailers and online, create the raised leaves. The thick plastic allows the plaster compound to build up in the stencil openings. The leaf motif, rendered in the vibrant golden tones shown here, is great for rustic or casual spaces. If painting an entire wall doesn't fit your plans, try using this treatment on a border above a chair rail or on a small space in any area that needs a special accent.

SKILL LEVEL

Beginner

SPECIAL TOOLS

a. Large putty knife

b. Glaze medium

c. Mini roller with 6-inch roller covers

d. Lint-free cotton cloths

TOOLS

2-inch-wide low-tack painter's tape

Drop cloth

Stir sticks

Paint tray

Standard roller frame with 9-inch roller cover

2-inch tapered trim brush

Stencil, see Resources, page 190

Stencil adhesive

Venetian plaster compound tinted to match base-coat color

2 plastic containers with printed measurements

Mini roller paint tray

Plastic 3-gallon bucket

Fine grit sandpaper

PAINT

Semigloss latex for all colors

GOLDEN TAN FOR BASE COAT

RED-BROWN FOR GLAZE COAT

LEAF GREEN FOR GLAZE COAT

Raised-Texture Stencil

INSTRUCTIONS

Mask ceiling, baseboards, and trim with painter's tape. Paint the entire wall in the golden tan base-coat color. Paint two coats if necessary. Leave tape on; let the paint dry overnight.

Using a plastic container with printed measurements, measure and mix 4 parts glaze to 1 part red-brown paint. In a second plastic container, measure and mix 4 parts glaze to 1 part leaf green paint.

Fill a 3-gallon bucket half full of clean water for rinsing lint-free cotton cloths.

1

Spray the back of the leaf stencil with stencil adhesive. Apply the stencil to the wall and firmly smooth the stencil in place. This will ensure that all areas have adhered well to create a tight seal around the edges of the design. Pick up a mound of tinted Venetian plaster compound on the putty knife. Holding the putty knife at an oblique (almost parallel) angle to the surface, use light pressure to press the material into the stencil openings. Remove the excess material from the trowel and then scrape lightly over the design to remove the excess compound down to the level of the stencil.

2

Carefully lift the stencil from one corner to remove it from the wall. Try to avoid sliding it and smearing the wet compound. If any little ridges appear around the edges of the design, do not try to repair them while the compound is wet. Wait until it has dried, then lightly sand with fine-grit sandpaper. Clean the stencil between each use by laying it on a flat surface and using the putty knife to scrape off the excess compound. Wipe off any material that may have been deposited on the back of the stencil as well. Continue to apply leaves as desired. The leaves on the wall shown on page 129 are placed in a heavy concentration at the top of the wall. They are placed farther apart as they drift down the wall to simulate leaves gently falling to the ground. Let dry.

TIP

For even more drama on the leaves, try dry-brushing highlight colors such as ivory or metallic gold over them using a small stiff-bristle flat artist's brush.

Single overlay stencils cut from thick stencil plastic work best for this technique.

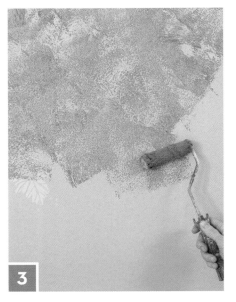

3

Pour some of the red-brown glaze mixture into the mini roller paint tray and lightly load the mini roller with glaze. Lightly roll the glaze onto the wall, allowing the roller to skip as you roll to create a random pattern of coverage.

4

Working quickly while the glaze is still wet, dampen a piece of lint-free cotton cloth with water and wring it out thoroughly. Loosely bunch the cloth and begin to dab and smudge the wet glaze mixture to remove some of the glaze and create a mottled appearance. As the cloth becomes saturated with glaze, rinse and wring it out again.

5

Gently wipe any glaze off the leaves before the glaze dries. Working one area at a time, finish glazing the wall. Let dry.

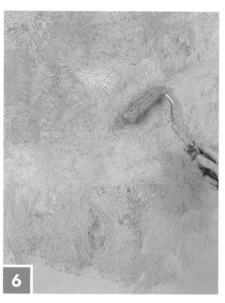

6

Repeat Step 3 using the leaf green glaze mixture. Use this glaze color sparingly so that the base-coat color and the red-brown glaze color remain visible.

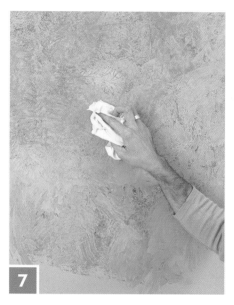

7

While the glaze is still wet, pat and blend, making sure you leave areas where the base coat and red-brown glaze color show through. Again gently wipe any glaze off the leaves before it dries. Working one area at a time, finish glazing the wall. Let dry.

8

After the glazing step is complete, stand back and evaluate the results. Add more red-brown glaze and leaf green glaze as desired.

TIP

The amount of tinted Venetian plaster compound you apply will yield varying results. Thin applications will create low relief while heavy applications will give a more dimensional result. Heavy applications will also reveal slight cracks when dry. This adds to the rustic appearance and creates a dramatic effect.

If you apply the compound heavily to achieve cracks in the leaves, be sure to allow the red-brown glaze mixture to seep into the crevices. Gently wipe off the surface of the leaves but leave the glaze in the cracks to create an antique look.

SKILL LEVEL
Intermediate

SPECIAL TOOLS
a. Crafts knife

b. Self-healing cutting mat

c. Stencil adhesive

d. Medium-size stenciling brush

a.

b.

c.

d.

TOOLS
2-inch-wide low-tack painter's tape

Drop cloth

Stir sticks

Paint tray

Standard roller frame with 9-inch roller cover

2-inch tapered trim brush

Chalk

Stencil patterns, pages 184–185

Stencil plastic

Fine-tip marker

Paper towels

Artist's liner brush

Sponge

Tape

PAINT
Semigloss latex for light olive green base coat, acrylic paint for all other colors

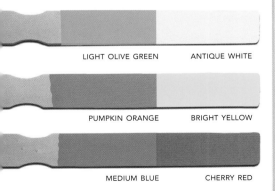

LIGHT OLIVE GREEN   ANTIQUE WHITE

PUMPKIN ORANGE   BRIGHT YELLOW

MEDIUM BLUE   CHERRY RED

Make Your Own Stencil

Fabric patterns are a great source of inspiration when planning a room's decor. With that inspiration and sheets of blank stencil plastic, you can make stencils and use them to give your walls a truly custom treatment. The fanciful flower-adorned tree on the narrow wall below repeats the colors and folksy style of the chair's fabric. Pattern elements for this motif are included in the patterns section beginning on page 184. You can enlarge the pattern to the desired size at a copy center or draw your own to assure a custom fit for the tree and its branches. Translucent stencil plastic, available at crafts retailers, is used to make the stencil. Using a crafts knife to cut the traced openings makes the job easy. The same process applies to any fabric-inspired motif. Simply pick the design elements you like from your fabric, enlarge to the desired size, and create one-of-a-kind stencils.

INSTRUCTIONS

Mask ceiling, baseboards, and trim with painter's tape. Paint the entire wall in the light olive green base-coat color. Paint two coats if necessary. Leave tape on; let the paint dry overnight.

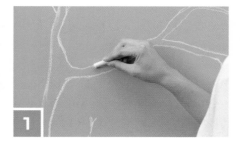

Use chalk to draw a tree image onto the wall to fit your space, referring to the photo opposite as a guide. Use a damp sponge to erase mistakes if necessary.

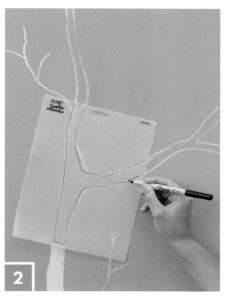

Tape a piece of stencil plastic onto the wall and use a fine-tip marker to trace portions of the tree trunk and branches. Start at the base of the tree and work your way up to the ends of the branches. In some cases a branch stencil may be flipped over to be used in a different area.

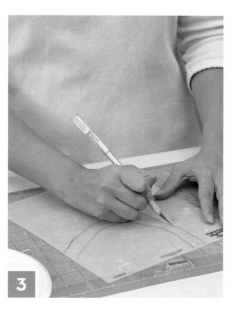

Lay the traced stencil plastic on a self-healing cutting mat. Use a crafts knife to cut out the design. Use a clean new blade in the crafts knife to yield crisp lines. Change the blade as needed. Cut out all trunk and branch stencils.

Trace and then cut out all flower stencils. Use the patterns provided or design your own based on inspiration from your fabric. Some flowers shown are composed of different colors. Cut an overlay for each color.

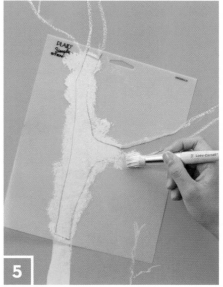

Spray the backside of the stencil with stencil adhesive. Apply the stencil to the wall and firmly smooth the stencil in place. Dip a medium-size stenciling brush into a small amount of antique white paint and blot the excess paint onto a paper towel. Use a gentle circular or light tapping motion to fill in the stencil openings. Start at the bottom of the tree trunk and move up toward the branches. Stencil the branches last.

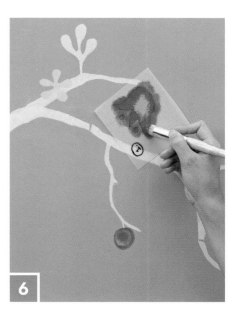

Stencil the flowers, one overlay at a time, as you designed them. Add final handpainted details as desired using an artist's liner brush.

SPECIAL TOOLS

a. Glaze medium

b. Lint-free cotton cloths

c. Stencil roller

a.

b.

c.

PAINT

Semigloss latex for base coat and glaze coat, acrylic paint for stamping

PALE YELLOW-GREEN FOR BASE COAT

YELLOW-GREEN FOR GLAZE COAT

ANTIQUE WHITE ACRYLIC FOR STAMPING

TOOLS

2-inch-wide low-tack painter's tape

Drop cloth

Stir sticks

Paint tray

Standard roller frame with 9-inch roller cover

2-inch tapered trim brush

Plastic container with printed measurements

Plastic 3-gallon bucket

Copy of the stamp pattern, page 187

Pencil

Scissors

1-inch-thick plexiglass, cut slightly larger than motif

Masking tape

Three 9×12-inch sheets of adhesive-back crafts foam, 2 mil thick

Size 12, $\frac{5}{16}$-inch, leather punch

Hammer

Cardboard

Disposable plate

Geometric Stamp

A simple stamped-on dot motif adds a sassy graphic note to the color-washed wall below. The custom stamp is made from punched-out dots of crafts foam adhered to a block of 1-inch-thick plexiglass. A leather punch and hammer are used to make the dots. Plexiglass, available at home centers and glass supply retailers, can be cut to order in any size. Using plexiglass to make custom stamps has two advantages: First its rigid composition allows you to apply firm pressure when stamping, yielding a crisp impression, and second because it is transparent, you can easily align the stamp motif exactly where you want it before pressing it to the surface you're decorating.

INSTRUCTIONS

Mask ceiling, baseboards, and trim with painter's tape. Paint the entire wall in the pale yellow-green base-coat color. Paint two coats if necessary. Leave tape on; let the paint dry overnight.

Using a plastic container with printed measurements, measure and mix 4 parts glaze to 1 part yellow-green paint.

Fill a 3-gallon bucket half full of clean water for rinsing lint-free cotton cloths.

1

Bunch a damp piece of soft, lint-free cloth and dip it into the glaze mixture. Wash the glaze onto the wall using a circular motion to create a softly mottled effect. Use a trim brush for corners and around the molding, then go over the surface with the cloth to remove brushstrokes. Let dry. Repeat the glaze application to create a second layer for more visual depth.

2

Peel the backing off two sheets of crafts foam and layer both sheets onto the third sheet, sticky sides down, with the third sheet's backing intact and on the bottom. Put the layered foam under a weight for approximately one hour to secure the bond. Place the bonded stack of crafts foam on top of a cardboard sheet and punch out dots using the leather punch and hammer.

3

Peel the protective backing off the plexiglass and place the plexiglass over one copy of the dot motif pattern, centering the design. Tape the pattern to the backside of the block so it can be seen through the plexiglass. Peel the adhesive backing from the dots and adhere them to the plexiglass one at a time using the pattern on the backside of the plexiglass as a guide.

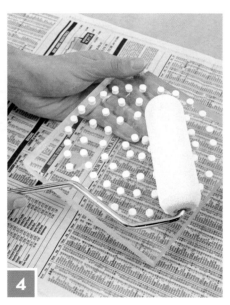

4

Pour a small amount of antique white paint onto a disposable plate. Using the stencil roller, apply paint to the surface of the stamp.

5

Press the stamp onto the wall using firm pressure, starting the first row approximately 6 inches from the ceiling and placing rows 6 inches apart. Remove the stamp without sliding it. Stamp one horizontal row at a time, staggering each row.

Textured Age Wash

Perfect for walls that are in less-than-perfect condition, the age-washed-texture technique imparts a dramatic backdrop for vintage furnishings. The four-step process requires three days to complete because of drying time needed for the texture compound and base coat of color. Untinted Venetian plaster compound, available at home centers, is applied for a texture base. The width of the putty knife or trowel you use and the amount of compound you apply determine the pattern and texture. Heavy applications of texture compound will crack as the compound dries. If you don't want cracks, use a wide trowel to apply a thin layer of compound. A base coat of color followed with a glaze top coat completes the process. Try this technique for an old-world European effect.

SKILL LEVEL

Beginner

SPECIAL TOOLS

a. Large putty knife

b. Glaze medium

c. Mini roller frame with 6-inch roller cover

d. Lint-free cotton cloths

a.

b.

c.

d.

TOOLS

Low-tack painter's tape

Drop cloth

Stir sticks

Paint tray

Standard roller frame with 9-inch roller cover

2-inch tapered trim brush

Untinted Venetian plaster compound

Plastic container with printed measurements

2 large plastic buckets

PAINT

Satin latex for all colors

PRIMER

PALE YELLOW FOR BASE COAT

ORANGE FOR GLAZE COAT

INSTRUCTIONS

Mask ceiling, baseboards, and trim with painter's tape. Paint the entire wall in primer. Paint two coats if necessary. Leave tape on; let the primer dry overnight.

1 Load a wide putty knife or trowel with untinted Venetian plaster compound. Spread plaster onto the wall in a random crosshatch pattern.

2 Occasionally lift and turn the putty knife to create variations in the texture. Allow to dry overnight.

3 Use the standard paint roller to base-coat the entire textured wall with pale yellow. Paint two coats if necessary. Let dry.

4 Using a plastic container with printed measurements, measure 4 parts glaze medium to 1 part orange paint into a clean bucket. Mix enough glaze for the entire project so the intensity of the glaze color is consistent. The total amount of glaze mixture should equal the amount of base-coat color applied for one-coat coverage (see page 13). Fill another bucket half full of clean water for rinsing lint-free cloths. Starting at the top of the wall, use a trim brush to cut in the glaze mixture, then use the mini roller to roll the orange glaze mixture onto an irregularly shaped 4-foot-square section of the wall.

5 Immediately wipe off the excess glaze mixture using a dampened lint-free cotton cloth, allowing the glaze to settle into the recessed areas. Use a clean area of the dampened cotton cloth to gently pat the wet glaze to blend and smooth out the color. Turn to a clean area of the dampened cotton cloth and gently wipe off some of the highest spots to reveal additional highlights. Move to an adjacent area and repeat rolling on the orange glaze mixture and wiping it off until the entire wall is completed. Remove all tape; allow to dry.

Faux Venetian Plaster

Multiple layers of paint, applied with a plastic trowel, simulate the look of worn plaster in the living room, opposite. The soft palette of blue and blue-green hues accented with creamy yellow makes a statement that packs a painterly punch in the modern space. The paint colors, blended while wet, combine to create a variety of tones and patterns. The color scheme shown here works well for a contemporary space but try mellow neutral or earthy tones of gold or terra-cotta for an old-world look. When choosing a color scheme for your wall, start with one very light and two medium to light values from the same paint sample strip, then add one or two highlight colors in a complementary hue.

SKILL LEVEL

Intermediate

SPECIAL TOOLS

a. Paint trays with liners

b. Mini roller

c. 8-inch-wide plastic trowel

a.

b.

c.

TOOLS

Low-tack painter's tape

Drop cloth

Stir sticks

Paint tray

Standard roller frame with 9-inch roller cover

2-inch tapered trim brush

PAINT

Semigloss latex for all colors

PALE BLUE FOR BASE COAT

LIGHT BLUE FOR LIGHT VALUE

MEDIUM BLUE-GREEN FOR DARK VALUE

PALE YELLOW FOR LIGHT ACCENTS

Faux Venetian Plaster

INSTRUCTIONS

Mask ceiling, baseboards, and trim with painter's tape. Paint the entire wall in the pale blue base-coat color. Paint two coats if necessary. Leave tape on; let the paint dry overnight.

1

To set up the paint colors, pour light blue, medium blue, and pale yellow paint into separate paint trays with liners.

2

Use the mini roller to roll light blue paint onto the wall, covering a 2-foot-wide section from ceiling to floor.

3

Working quickly while the light blue paint is still wet, dip one side of the trowel into light blue paint, then dip the other into medium blue paint so there are two colors on the trowel. The colors will mix as you apply paint to the wall.

4

With the medium blue loaded side of the trowel facing the wall, start near the ceiling, and using firm pressure, apply the paint with long vertical strokes. Immediately flip the trowel over so the light blue side is facing the wall and make another stroke on top of the first medium blue stroke, using firm pressure to create streaks and blend the colors. Work down the wall, picking up more of each paint color as needed.

5

Dip the trowel into light blue only. Working quickly use very light pressure to skim the surface of the wall, skipping some areas and depositing paint on other areas to create highlights.

6

Dip the trowel into the pale yellow paint and, with the trowel held nearly flat against the wall, use very light pressure to skim along the surface from ceiling to floor, depositing the accent color in a random pattern.

7

Roll light blue paint onto an adjacent area. Create an uneven edge with the roller where it abuts the previously painted section to avoid harsh lines where the sections meet.

8

Continue to paint the entire wall one section at a time, repeating Steps 3–7. Let dry.

9

After the wall is complete, stand back and evaluate the result. Add light blue, medium blue, and pale yellow as needed until the desired look is achieved.

Variation A

Give plain off-white walls a mellow, aged appearance by troweling on closely related light-tone hues of tan, beige, and pale copper.

Variation B

A warm terra-cotta and gold color combination gives a timeworn Tuscan villa atmosphere to walls in rooms used for entertaining.

Torn-Paper Appliqué

Create subtle texture that mimics the timeworn look of walls layered over decades with coats of plaster. The technique works well in hiding flaws and imperfections on older walls. Torn pieces of craft paper applied to the wall produce the initial texture. The size of the paper pieces used determines the final pattern. The pieces shown opposite are approximately 6×6 inches. For more texture apply two or more layers of paper. Base-coat hues of brown, gold, and terra-cotta yield an earthy look that complements a rustic decorating style. Try more vibrant hues for contemporary spaces.

SKILL LEVEL

Beginner

SPECIAL TOOLS

a. Brown craft paper

b. Brown gel stain

c. Lint-free cotton cloths

a.

b.

c.

TOOLS

Low-tack painter's tape

Drop cloth

Stir sticks

Paint tray

Standard roller frame with 9-inch roller cover

2-inch tapered trim brush

Wallpaper paste

Mini roller frame with 6-inch roller cover

Wallpaper smoothing tool

PAINT

Semigloss latex for top coat

PRIMER FOR BASE COAT

DARK TAN FOR TOP COAT

INSTRUCTIONS

Mask ceiling, baseboards, and trim with painter's tape. Paint the entire wall in primer. Paint two coats if necessary. Leave tape on; let the primer dry overnight.

Tear brown craft paper into irregularly shaped pieces of similar size.

Use the mini roller to apply wallpaper paste onto a few pieces of the torn craft paper. One at a time place them on the wall, slightly overlapping them.

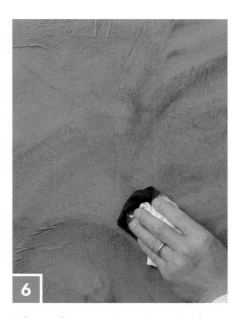

Use the wallpaper smoothing tool to smooth the paper pieces and remove excess wallpaper paste. Let dry.

With the painter's tape still in place, base-coat the entire wall with dark tan. Paint two coats if necessary. Leave tape on; let the paint dry overnight.

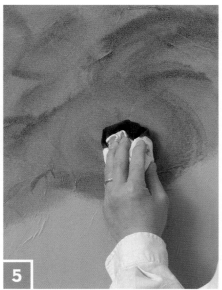

Loosely bunch a piece of clean lint-free cotton cloth and dip into gel stain. Rub the stain onto the wall in a circular motion. Cover a 4-foot-square irregularly shaped area.

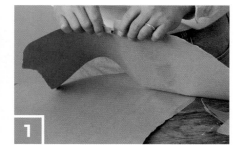

Rub over the same area again in a circular motion to even out the stain color. Allow the stain to accumulate in the joints between the paper pieces. Move to an adjacent area and repeat the process until the entire wall is completed. As one piece of cloth becomes saturated with stain, discard it and use a clean one. Remove all tape; let dry. Follow the manufacturer's instructions for proper use and cleanup of oil-base products.

Sponged Wash

The worn appearance of old stucco walls, reminiscent of a Tuscan villa, is easy to create. The technique, accomplished using closely related glaze hues and a large natural sponge, imparts mellow, aged character to walls but won't overpower furnishings. Using three graduating tones of color—one pale-, one light-, and one medium-value hue—picked from the lightest choices on the same paint sample strip is the easiest way to select coordinating colors. When choosing a sponge look for one that has an area with small openings to create a fine, speckled pattern rather than a large, heavy pattern. Experiment using the sponge on a sample board until you are confident that you can achieve a soft, dappled effect.

SKILL LEVEL
Beginner

SPECIAL TOOLS
a. Glaze medium

b. Disposable plastic plates

c. Natural sponge

a.

b.

c.

TOOLS
2-inch-wide low-tack painter's tape

Drop cloth

Stir sticks

Paint tray

Standard roller frame with 9-inch roller cover

2-inch tapered trim brush

2 plastic containers with printed measurements

Plastic 3-gallon bucket

PAINT
Satin latex for all colors

GOLDEN TAN FOR BASE COAT

ANTIQUE WHITE FOR LIGHT GLAZE COAT

DARK GOLD FOR DARKER GLAZE COAT

INSTRUCTIONS

Mask ceiling, baseboards, and trim with painter's tape. Paint the entire wall in the golden tan base-coat color. Paint two coats if necessary. Leave tape on; let dry overnight.

In a plastic container mix 4 parts glaze to 1 part dark gold paint. In a separate plastic container, mix 4 parts glaze to 1 part antique white paint. Pour each glaze into separate disposable plastic plates. Fill a 3-gallon plastic bucket with clean water for rinsing the sponge.

Wet a large natural sponge and wring it out thoroughly. Dip the sponge into the dark gold glaze mixture. Lightly tap the loaded sponge onto a piece of drop cloth to even out the glaze mixture distribution in the sponge.

To apply the glaze mixture, lightly tap the sponge onto the wall, constantly turning the sponge as you tap, to create a random dappled pattern. Sponge the glaze mixture onto a 4-foot-square irregularly shaped area, covering about 80 percent of the golden tan base-coat color.

Rinse the sponge and wring it out thoroughly. Repeating Step 2, load the clean damp sponge with the antique white glaze mixture and apply to the wall. First cover the spaces left uncovered with the dark gold glaze mixture, then go over some of the dark gold glazed areas as well. Try to cover about 70 percent of the area you are working.

Rinse and wring out the sponge, then reload with the dark gold glaze mixture. Using very light pressure to achieve a very small dappled pattern, sponge on more of the dark gold glaze mixture.

Repeating Step 4, reload the sponge with the antique white glaze mixture and sponge on highlights. Move to an adjacent area and continue to sponge glazes onto the wall until the entire area is covered. Remove all tape; let dry.

SKILL LEVEL
Beginner

SPECIAL TOOLS
a. Glaze medium
b. Newspaper

TOOLS
Low-tack painter's tape

Drop cloth

Stir sticks

Paint tray

Standard roller frame with 9-inch roller cover

2-inch tapered trim brush

2 plastic containers with printed measurements

Large plastic bucket

PAINT
Semigloss latex for all colors

WHITE FOR BASE COAT

DARK GOLD FOR GLAZE COAT

DARK BROWN FOR FINAL AGING GLAZE COAT

Aged Frottage

Bring the character of sun-drenched stucco that's been aged over time to walls in rooms that call for a casual, rustic backdrop. The cornerstone of this look employs a traditional technique known as frottage. The word, frottage, from the French word *frotter,* means "to rub." A sheet of newspaper is pressed onto the wall over a wet rolled-on top coat of glaze and rubbed so that it wrinkles. The paper absorbs moisture from the glaze mixture and, when removed, reveals a random pattern of light and dark areas. To enhance the effect a dark brown glaze mixture is randomly dabbed on and rubbed with a bunched piece of newsprint to soften and blend the color. Some of the ink from the newsprint transfers to the wall and is absorbed into the glaze coats slightly, altering the colors and adding to the aged effect. Earthtone hues produce the best results.

INSTRUCTIONS

Mask ceiling, baseboards, and trim with painter's tape. Paint the entire wall in the white base-coat color. Paint two coats if necessary. Leave tape on; let the paint dry overnight.

Using a plastic container with printed measurements, measure 4 parts glaze to 1 part dark gold paint into a clean bucket. Mix enough glaze for the entire project so the intensity of the glaze color is consistent from panel to panel. The total amount of glaze mixture should equal the amount of base-coat color applied for one-coat coverage (see page 13). In a second plastic container, mix 4 parts glaze to 1 part dark brown paint. Unless your room is very large you will not need a large quantity of the dark brown glaze mixture.

1

Use the paint roller to apply a layer of dark gold glaze mixture over an irregularly shaped 3-foot-square section of the wall.

2

Working quickly while the glaze mixture is still wet, lay a single sheet of newspaper over the glaze area. Use both hands to press the paper onto the wall, allowing wrinkles to form in the newspaper as it soaks up the moisture from the glaze.

3

Carefully remove the newspaper from the wall and discard. Repeat the process across the entire wall, using a new piece of newspaper each time you work a new section. As you move from section to section, roll the glaze on well beyond the edge of the newspaper to ensure there are no hard lines where the sections meet. Let dry. Go over any areas a second time if desired to blend the edges or vary the color. Let dry.

4

Use the tapered trim brush to dab dark brown glaze sparingly onto a 2-foot-square area.

5

While the glaze is still wet, use a crumpled piece of newspaper to dab and rub the glaze to blend. Remove all tape; let dry.

SKILL LEVEL

Beginner

SPECIAL TOOLS

a. Level with printed ruler

b. 2-inch-wide low-tack painter's tape

c. Mini roller

d. Crackle medium

a.

b.

c.

d.

TOOLS

Drop cloth

Stir sticks

Paint tray

Standard roller frame with 9-inch roller cover

2-inch tapered trim brush

Colored pencil

2-inch-wide chip brush

Crafts knife

Porcelain Crackle

Crackled paint creates a rustic, country, or vintage look and also works well with contemporary or modern decorating styles. The crackle-paint framed panels in the entryway below are a perfect accompaniment to contemporary, Asian-style furniture and accessories. Crackle medium, available at crafts retailers, is the key ingredient for this technique. It is applied between two layers of paint. The crackle medium causes the top coat of paint to shrink as it dries, creating cracks that reveal the base coat color underneath. Experiment with color combinations and try reversing base-coat and top-coat colors to see the dramatic difference that can be produced with the same color scheme.

PAINT

Semigloss latex for all colors

TAN FOR WALL BASE COAT

DARK TAN FOR CRACKLE BASE COAT

ANTIQUE WHITE FOR CRACKLE TOP COAT

INSTRUCTIONS

Mask ceiling, baseboards, and trim with painter's tape. Paint the entire wall in the tan base-coat color. Paint two coats if necessary. Remove tape; let the paint dry overnight.

To begin laying out the panels, measure and mark the wall with an upper and lower mark for each vertical line. Use the long level and colored pencil to draw in vertical lines to connect the upper and lower marks at each interval. The level will ensure that the lines stay vertical and parallel to one another. Measure and mark the wall at intervals for the horizontal lines. Use the long level and colored pencil to draw in horizontal lines to complete the panel layout. The right and left panels are about 24×40 inches and the center panel is 34×40 inches.

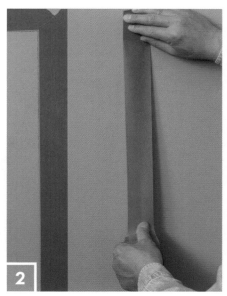

Tape off all panels with the low-tack painter's tape.

Use the mini paint roller to paint each taped-off panel in the dark tan crackle base coat. Do not remove the tape; let the paint dry.

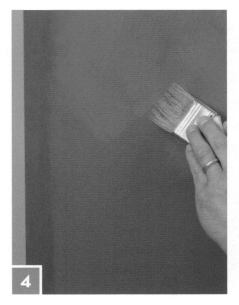

Use the 2-inch-wide chip brush to apply crackle medium in crosshatching motions; let dry.

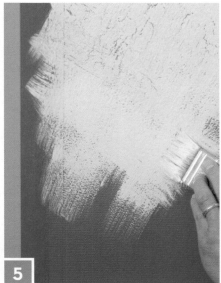

Use the chip brush to apply the antique white top coat, moving from left to right and top to bottom as quickly as possible in crosshatching motions. Cracking will occur quickly. Do not overlap or rebrush the top coat of paint after the paint has started to crack. Touch-ups will be obvious and will not crack again.

Remove the tape immediately after applying the top coat and before the paint completely dries. If the paint should start to lift off when removing the tape, use a crafts knife to carefully score through the paint along the edges of the tape. Let dry. Repeat for each panel.

Simple Mural

Painted using a limited palette, a wall mural makes a sophisticated statement in a traditional dining room or entryway. Basic techniques for painting clouds, pastures of grass, trees, and pools of water combine to create pastoral scenes. Once mastered the elements may be used in many ways to create a variety of vistas. Oil-base paints work well for painting murals because they dry slowly, allowing time for painting large areas and blending colors together. If you prefer to use latex paints you can slow the drying process and increase the paint's workability by adding paint conditioner or special retarding mediums to your paint colors. If you're a novice painter, practice each design element on sample boards.

SKILL LEVEL

Intermediate

SPECIAL TOOLS

a. Disposable plastic plates

b. Artist's oil paints

c. Chip brushes

d. Artist's brushes

a.

b.

c.

d.

TOOLS

Low-tack painter's tape

Drop cloth

Stir sticks

Paint tray

Standard roller frame with 9-inch roller cover

2-inch tapered trim brush

Level with printed ruler

Light brown color pencil

Palette knife

Boiled linseed oil

Mineral spirits

Wide-mouth glass jar with lid

Lint-free cotton cloths

PAINT

Satin latex for base coat, artist's oil paints for all other colors

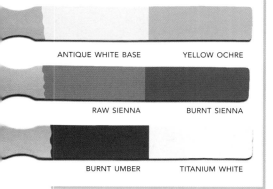

ANTIQUE WHITE BASE   YELLOW OCHRE

RAW SIENNA   BURNT SIENNA

BURNT UMBER   TITANIUM WHITE

Freehand Fun

Simple Mural

INSTRUCTIONS

Mask ceiling, baseboards, and trim with painter's tape. Paint the entire wall in the antique white base-coat color. Paint two coats if necessary. Remove tape; let the paint dry overnight.

1 To mark a line for the chair rail, use a level and light color pencil to measure and mark a line 30 inches from the baseboard. Draw a horizon line halfway between the ceiling and chair rail. To indicate the far water's edge, draw another line halfway between the horizon line and the chair rail line. To indicate the foreground water's edge, draw a line halfway between the far water's edge and the chair rail line.

2 For a painting medium pour equal amounts of boiled linseed oil and mineral spirits into a wide-mouth glass jar. Squeeze lima bean-size piles of yellow ocher, raw sienna, burnt sienna, burnt umber, and titanium white onto a plastic disposable plate. Dip the 2-inch-wide trim brush into the painting medium and brush a very thin coat onto the entire sky area above the horizon line. Pick up a small amount of yellow ocher and streak it onto the sky area. Brush out the color until the sky becomes completely covered with a very thin layer of transparent color. Allow some areas to remain darker to give the sky depth and interest. Do not clean the brush.

3 Loosely bunch a piece of lint-free cotton cloth and, using a circular motion, remove the color in several areas to create billowy clouds. If you dislike the results, brush back over the area with the trim brush to spread out the color and repeat wiping out clouds until you're satisfied.

4 Touch one corner of the trim brush into the yellow ochre and tap the loaded brush onto a clean disposable plastic plate to distribute the color evenly in the corner of the bristles. With the loaded corner of the brush against the horizon line, use a light-pressure pouncing motion to apply foliage to the background trees.

5 Without cleaning the brush, touch the yellow-ocher-loaded corner into raw sienna, tap onto the plate, and, with the loaded corner against the horizon line, use a pouncing motion to apply shading to the background tree foliage. Keep most of the raw sienna color at the base of the tree line.

Dip the brush into the painting medium and brush across the middle-ground area from the horizon line to the far water's edge. Brush on additional raw sienna at the water's edge for shading.

To create tufts of grass, make short vertical strokes at random in the middle-ground area.

Use a palette knife to mix painting medium with burnt umber to thin the pigment to a brushing consistency. Load a round artist's brush and use the pattern on page 186 as a guide to paint the background tree trunks.

Repeating Step 4, load the trim brush and apply yellow ocher foliage to the middle-ground trees. Continue to build foliage shading by separately applying raw sienna, then burnt sienna, then burnt umber. As you apply each paint color, the pigments will blend and soften the effect. Be careful not to overblend.

Wipe the trim brush thoroughly on a clean lint-free cloth. Dip the tips of the brush bristles into the painting medium and brush across the entire water area to moisten the surface. Using the same color progression used for the foliage in Step 9, paint a line of low foliage along the far water's edge. To create a reflection place the bristle tips horizontally at the bottom edge of the foliage and make short downward strokes, pulling the color down into the water area.

Wipe the trim brush thoroughly, and lightly brush horizontally through the water reflection to soften and create a shimmering effect.

12 Thin titanium white with painting medium and use the artist's brush to paint white ripple lines along the water's edge.

13 Use the artist's brush and thinned burnt umber to paint tree branches, twigs in the bushes, and grass clusters.

14 Stand back and evaluate the painting, then use the trim brush to pounce yellow ocher and titanium white highlights as desired on the foliage. Make short, upward vertical strokes to highlight the grass areas. Dip the trim brush into painting medium and moisten the foreground grass area from the foreground water's edge to the chair rail line. Complete the foreground grass, trees, and bushes by repeating Steps 6–9. Let dry.

Variation A

Varying tones of blue-green were used for this tone-on-tone landscape. Here the mural was painted on canvas hung to suggest an old-world tapestry. The border was handpainted but there are many scroll border stencils available online and at crafts stores that would make a quick and easy substitute.

Variation B

Large foreground trees that extend from just above the chair rail to the ceiling give a sense of depth and distance while creating a feeling that the viewer is standing in a grove of trees. With the emphasis on the foreground, the background drifts into the misty distance. A limited palette of soft greens and browns keeps the overall effect from being overpowering and blends the mural with the room's color scheme.

SKILL LEVEL

Intermediate

SPECIAL TOOLS

a. Disposable
   plastic plates

b. Artist's
   paintbrushes

a.

b.

TOOLS

Low-tack
painter's tape

Drop cloth

Stir sticks

Paint tray

Standard roller
frame with 9-inch
roller cover

2-inch tapered
trim brush

String

Pushpin

Colored pencil

Compass

Graph paper

Lint-free cotton
cloths

Shampoo

PAINT

Satin latex for base coat, acrylic crafts
paint for circles

DARK BROWN FOR BASE COAT

LIGHT BLUE FOR CIRCLES

Geometrics

Widely used on textiles and decorative accessories of all kinds, geometric motifs prove to be immensely popular elements in modern and contemporary design trends. The pattern of intersecting circles, inspired by the fabric used on a chair and painted on the wall of the family room below adds a distinctive graphic element to the room's decor. A simple homemade compass creates the circle patterns. To make the tool tie one end of a length of string around the head of a pushpin and the opposite end of the string around a pencil. The lines, painted in a sketchy, casual style, contribute to the artistic look so don't worry if your hand is not rock steady. A little variation in line width and paint coverage only adds to the effect. For a bold impact use widely contrasting colors like the combination shown here. For a softer look use tone-on-tone hues.

INSTRUCTIONS

Mask ceiling, baseboards, and trim with painter's tape. Paint the entire wall in the dark brown base-coat color. Paint two coats if necessary. Remove tape; let dry overnight.

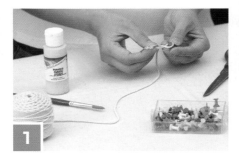

Make a scale drawing of your wall on graph paper. Make a compass for each size circle you wish to draw. To do this, measure and cut a length of string 6 inches longer than the diameter of each desired circle size. Tie one end of each length of string around the plastic end of a pushpin. Tie the opposite end of the string around a colored pencil.

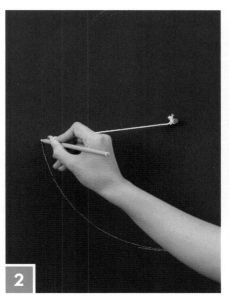

Insert the pushpin into the wall at the center of the desired circle. Holding the pencil at a 90-degree angle to the wall, stretch the string taut and draw the circle onto the wall.

Draw the circles one at a time, standing back to evaluate the placement as you proceed. If you wish to change the placement of a circle, the pencil mark can be washed off using a damp, lint-free cotton cloth and a bit of shampoo.

Pour a small amount of light blue acrylic paint onto a disposable plastic plate. To slightly thin the paint for painting lines, dip a round artist's brush into clean water and mix into one edge of the puddle of light blue paint. Load the brush and roll the handle between your fingers to form the brush bristles into a fine point.

Follow the drawn lines to paint each circle. Reload the brush as needed. To connect at the end of the line you are painting, slightly overlap the paint and continue to paint along the circle.

Avoid applying a solid coverage of paint for this design. A casual sketched-on look is more varied and interesting. Continue to paint the circles until the entire design is completed.

SKILL LEVEL

Beginner

SPECIAL TOOLS

a. Disposable
   plastic plates

b. Artist's
   brushes

a.

b.

TOOLS

Low-tack
painter's tape

Drop cloth

Stir sticks

Paint tray

Standard roller
frame with 9-inch
roller cover

2-inch tapered
trim brush

Tape measure

Light color chalk

Green color
pencil

Tracing paper

PAINT

Satin latex for base coat, acrylic crafts
paint for other colors

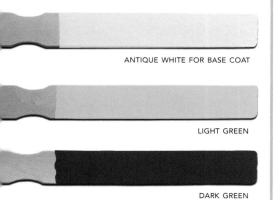

ANTIQUE WHITE FOR BASE COAT

LIGHT GREEN

DARK GREEN

Vines & Leaves

Realistic, stylized, or in bold silhouettes, botanical art is a staple today in decorating. Inspiration is everywhere you look—on fabric, wallcoverings, and decor accessories. Gently curving vines, casually sketched on at 12-inch intervals, create the basic structure for the motif on the headboard opposite. Simple leaves branch off each vine to complete the motif. You needn't worry about painting the leaves precisely. A casual, sketchy painting style works best so relax and have fun with it.

Vines & Leaves

INSTRUCTIONS

Mask ceiling, baseboards, and trim with painter's tape. Paint the entire wall in the antique white base-coat color. Paint two coats if necessary. Remove tape; let the paint dry overnight.

1

Starting in one corner of the room or at the edge of the wall section to be painted, measure and use light-color chalk to mark the desired intervals for vine spacing. Using these marks as guides, draw an irregular, gently curving line for each vine stem. Use a green color pencil that can be easily covered with paint.

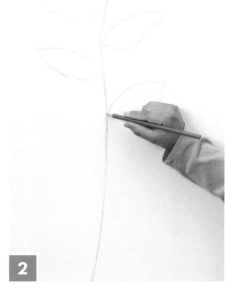

2

Trace the leaf patterns on page 187 onto tracing paper, enlarge them, and transfer the basic shapes onto the wall or use them as a guide to sketch your own leaves.

TIP

Study botanical subjects on wallpaper, fabric, or vintage art prints for motif inspiration. Make simple sketches first then enlarge to the desired size and use the enlargements as templates for the final design.

Base-coat walls with satin or semigloss paint before handpainting motifs. Mistakes are more easily scrubbed off these more nonporous surfaces.

3

Pour a small amount of light green acrylic paint onto a disposable plastic plate. Using a small round artist's paintbrush, base-coat the vines; let dry. If solid coverage is desired, apply two coats, letting the paint dry between coats.

4

Using a large round artist's brush, base-coat the leaves with light green paint; let dry.

5

Pour a small amount of dark green acrylic paint onto a disposable plastic plate. To slightly thin the paint for detail painting, dip a round artist's brush into clean water and mix into one edge of the puddle of dark green paint. Load the brush and roll the handle between your fingers to form the brush bristles into a fine point. In a hit-or-miss fashion, stroke the loaded brush down one side of each vine stem to indicate shading; let dry.

6

Stroke contour lines onto each leaf using a round artist's brush and dark green paint; let dry.

Variation A

Silhouettes are easy to paint and impart graphic punch to a room's decor. In this child's room the crib's bedding inspired the tree silhouette painted a few shades darker than the wall color. To get a similar look, start with a chalk-sketch tree trunk, then add branches. You can either create a leaf template to trace at the end of each branch or draw the leaves freehand for variety. Add a couple of plump birds to complete the look.

Variation B

The stylized leaf-and-vine motif on the wall in this dining room is based on a grid of graceful curves that interlock into a repeating pattern. To re-create this design make a scale drawing of the wall on graph paper and plot the vine repeats using a French curve template. Draw in the leaves for one complete repeat and create a template that can be transferred to the wall.

SKILL LEVEL

Advanced

SPECIAL TOOLS

a. Level with printed ruler

b. Disposable plastic plates

c. Artist's brushes

a.

b.

c.

TOOLS

Low-tack painter's tape

Drop cloth

Stir sticks

Paint tray

Standard roller frame with 9-inch roller cover

2-inch tapered trim brush

Flexible yardstick

Chalk

PAINT

Satin latex for base coat, acrylic crafts paint for detail

PALE GREEN FOR BASE COAT

WHITE

Strokes & Dots

Inspired by *mehndi*—the Indian tradition of ornamenting hands and feet with henna, the bedroom below features a wall decorated with a delicate pattern of repeating elements. At first glance the pattern looks complicated, but if you study the design further, you'll notice that it is laid out on a grid using groups of strokes and dots to build the motifs. A pattern of C and S shapes flows from a basic grid of dots applied in horizontal and vertical rows. Dot groupings and connecting lines fill in the design. Practice painting C and S shapes on a sample board until you're confident making the stroke patterns before you begin painting a wall.

INSTRUCTIONS

Mask ceiling, baseboards, and trim with painter's tape. Paint the entire wall in the pale green base-coat color. Paint two coats if necessary. Remove tape; let dry overnight.

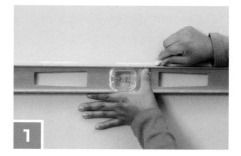

1

To begin laying out the design grid, first measure the total height of the wall in inches. Divide the total wall height by 12 to determine the number of horizontal repeats. Using a level and chalk, measure and mark the wall with horizontal lines at 12-inch intervals. The level will ensure that the lines stay parallel to one another.

2

Attach a flexible yardstick to the wall immediately above a chalk line. Pour a small amount of white acrylic paint onto a disposable plastic plate. Dip the end of an artist's brush handle into the paint and make one dot every 12 inches along the chalk line. Move the flexible yardstick as needed. Make dots at 12-inch intervals along each horizontal line on the entire wall.

3

Using the pattern on page 188 as a guide, make vertical rows of dots at each 12-inch interval along the horizontal rows of dots. Begin filling in the scroll designs on either side of each vertical row of dots.

4

Continue to fill in details, painting lines and making dots in repetitive groupings.

5

When painting the scrolls place the tip of the brush on the surface and apply pressure as you draw an "S" or "C" shape, then lift the brush as you come to the end of the curved stroke. Make a dot at each end of the shape.

6

Continue to fill in the design elements until the desired effect is achieved.

Freehand Flowers

Whimsical flowers, casually painted coloring book-style, ramp up a room's decor quickly and easily. Painted motifs add another dimension to a mix of patterns and tie a room's color scheme together at the same time. Using inspiration provided by patterns on decorative accessories or fabric is a great way to create templates for painting. Motifs, traced by hand or scanned on a computer, are easy to enlarge either on a computer or at a copy center.

SKILL LEVEL

Beginner

SPECIAL TOOLS

a. Disposable plastic plates

b. Artist's brushes

a.

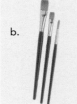

b.

TOOLS

Low-tack painter's tape

Drop cloth

Stir sticks

Paint tray

Standard roller frame with 9-inch roller cover

2-inch tapered trim brush

Red and green color pencils

PAINT

Satin latex for base coat, acrylic crafts paint for other colors

PALE PINK FOR BASE COAT

BRIGHT PINK

ORANGE

LIGHT GREEN

OLIVE GREEN

TIP

Paint flowers using hues that bring the room's color scheme to life. A variety of premixed colors is available packaged in handy 2-ounce squeeze bottles at arts and crafts stores.

Freehand Fun

Freehand Flowers

INSTRUCTIONS

Mask ceiling, baseboards, and trim with painter's tape. Paint the entire wall in the pale pink base-coat color. Paint two coats if necessary. Remove tape; let dry overnight.

TIP

Look at fabric and wallpaper designs for flower motif inspiration and color cues.

To create templates for painting, trace design elements and enlarge using a photocopier or computer.

1 Using the photo on page 165 as a guide for placement, make a light pencil mark to indicate the center of each flower. Trace the flower patterns on page 189, enlarge them, and transfer the basic shapes onto the wall or use them as a guide to sketch your own flowers. Use a red color pencil that can be easily covered with paint.

2 Add flower petals and other details as desired.

3 Use a green color pencil to draw a vertical gently curved line that extends from the bottom of each flower to the baseboard. Draw leaves on each side of the flower stem.

4 Pour small amounts of bright pink and orange acrylic paint onto a disposable plastic plate. Using a flat artist's brush that best fits the area, base-coat the flower centers on all round flowers; let dry. If solid coverage is desired, apply two coats, letting the paint dry between coats. Base-coat a few of the tulips with orange; let dry.

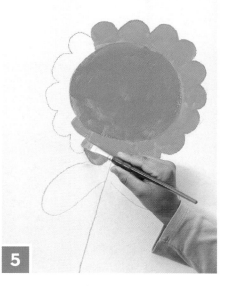

5 Paint the petals of the round flowers with orange. Use a wide flat brush for large petals and a small flat brush for small petals; let dry. Use a small round brush to paint detail lines on the round flower petals. Dip the end of a paintbrush handle into orange paint and make dots on some of the round flower centers. Use a small round brush to paint large pink dots on the orange tulips. Use a narrow flat brush to paint an orange scalloped edge on each pink tulip; let dry.

6

Pour small amounts of light green and olive green acrylic paint onto a disposable plastic plate. Base-coat each stem and all leaves with light green; let dry. Use a small round brush to paint olive green vein lines on each leaf; let dry.

Variation A

Fabric-inspired brightly colored tropical flowers casually drift across the wall in this girl's room. Using layers of solid colors gives a dimensional look. No shading or details are required for these flowers that pack a graphic tropical punch.

TIP

If you can't find a color to exactly match your color scheme, mix your own using crafts paints as a starting point. Since paints appear darker when they are dry, test each color before applying it on the wall by painting a swatch on a piece of cardboard that has been painted with the wall's base-coat color.

When working with acrylic crafts paints, add small amounts of water or specially formulated extender to the paint to improve workability. Since this type of paint dries quickly, pour out only small amounts onto the disposable plastic plate.

Variation A How-To

To create a basic layout for this design, lightly sketch a gently curving line horizontally along each wall to give the flower-and-leaf vine motif its basic structure. After painting the flowers use several green hues to paint the leaves.

Variation B

The bold, graphic flowers scattered along the upper wall in this loft-style girl's room were inspired by the room's chandeliers. To achieve a similar effect, trace any desired flower shapes and take the tracings to a copy center to enlarge. Use the copies as templates for painting.

3 Clever Combinations

In the same way that layering fabrics with different patterns and textures adds interest to a room's furnishings, so combining paint treatments on walls adds another layer of visual depth. Whether you duplicate one of the ideas in this chapter or use your imagination to create your own combinations, try using pairs of techniques to give your rooms one-of-a-kind style.

Stencil & Wallpaper

Sometimes when designing a decorating project, you can't find the exact combination of pattern, texture, and color that you envision in the materials available to you. By adding pattern to solid-ground wallpaper you can create a custom look that's a perfect fit for your personal style. The soft-hue grass cloth in the bedroom below is enhanced with stenciled Asian-style medallions that support both the room's textiles and furnishings.

When stenciling grass cloth, choose a stencil with plenty of graphic punch. Delicate designs will break up in the texture of the paper. To design placement on the wall, cut circles of craft paper and tape them in place, moving the elements until you achieve the desired look. Be sure to test your design on a scrap of wallpaper before stenciling on the wall.

Vertical stripe-paint wall treatments not only give rooms a greater sense of height visually, they also lend an atmosphere of sophistication to any decor. The myriad of possible stripe combinations is limited only by the imagination. Any standard wall painting technique gains an entirely new appearance when rendered in a striped pattern. And handpainting or stenciling within a striped pattern opens another world of possibilities.

Double Roller & Stripes

The freehand stripes painted on a foundation of mottled color give the wall in the bedroom below a modern take on a traditional motif. The base-coat pattern is applied using a double-roller kit available at home centers. Stripes are then measured and marked using a level and light color pencil before being handpainted with a round artist's brush.

Three shades of green create a monochromatic color scheme. Choose a color combination with mistake-proof results by picking three hues from the same color sample strip from a paint retailer.

Stencil & Stripes

A soft tone-on-tone palette combined with a contemporary floral stencil give the dining room wall below its modern style. The subtle color scheme and graphic pattern broken into stripes enhance the room's decor without overpowering it. A large allover wall stencil speeds up the job.

To produce the look first measure and mark the walls at intervals to create a pattern of wide and narrow stripes. Use a level to ensure lines are straight and plumb. After taping off the narrow stripes, stencil the first run starting at the ceiling. Letting the pattern bleed off the edges of the stripe gives the pattern its natural look.

The radiant shimmer of metallic paint gives an elegant finish to nearly any decorative technique. When metallic finishes are used to execute glaze techniques such as color-washing, dry-brushing, or sponge painting in combination with applied patterns such as stencils, stripes, or handpainting, the result is ramped-up style beyond the ordinary.

Metallic Glaze & Stencil

Small rooms with natural light are perfect candidates for metallic paint treatments because they catch and reflect the light differently throughout the day. Medallions stenciled with pearlescent white paint over a metallic gold-washed wall give the bathroom below upscale glamour. Because very little paint is used for this technique there is no need to purchase large quantities of metallic paints. Small bottles of metallic paints, purchased at a crafts retailer, go a long way.

For this look a wash of gold metallic paint is first washed on and then partially lifted off with sheets of unprinted newsprint paper. After the gold wash has dried, the medallion placements are plotted on the wall using a ruler and a level. The center of each medallion is marked with a dot of chalk before being stenciled with iridescent pearl paint.

Stripes & Dry-Brushed Metallic Gold

The traditional dining room below goes from elegant to opulent with tone-on-tone stripes above the chair rail and a gold metallic linen-weave technique below. Crisp white-paint woodwork frames the dramatic wall treatment and creates continuity with the furnishings, most of which are white.

Above the chair rail stripes are painted in the same hue but in two different sheens. The wall is first base-coated with flat-finish paint. Then alternating stripes get taped off and painted with semigloss paint in the same color. Below the chair rail a dark chocolate base coat is applied in flat-finish paint. Metallic gold is then dry-brushed on using short horizontal and vertical strokes.

Whether traditional, contemporary, or mod, flowers impart feminine ambience to any living space. Used with other decorative paint treatments, they give rooms an additional layer of visual texture and style in the way that layering fabric patterns adds interest to soft furnishings.

Stripes & Cottage Roses

Soft and sweet, the handpainted pink roses atop sunny stripes give the living room below its classic cottage style. In keeping with the casually brushed roses, the stripes are outlined with pinstripes in a slightly darker yellow tone.

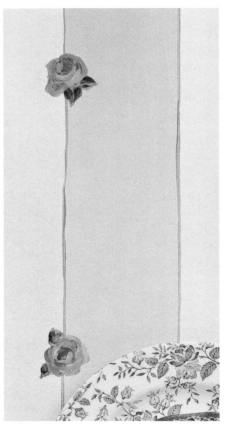

To get this look a base coat of antique white is applied first. A satin- or semigloss-finish paint works best for a base coat when decorating with handpainted embellishments because mistakes can be easily removed with a damp cloth. After the base coat has dried, alternating stripes are taped off and painted. A simple rose-and-leaf pattern is then lightly transferred onto the stripes at regular intervals and then freehand painted with acrylic paints using small artist's brushes. An artist's long liner brush is used to paint the pinstripes.

Blend & Stamped Flowers

The mod-style stamped pattern on the wall in this teen girl's room was inspired by the fabric motifs on the bed linens. Combined with a pounce-blended base coat of two pale pink hues, the result is a visually soft effect similar to printed fabric. The stamp is handmade from sheets of crafts foam adhered to a block of acrylic sheeting. See detailed instructions for making your own stamps on page 135.

When creating flower motifs keep in mind that simple graphic shapes work best for homemade stamps. For the wall's background of color, first choose three pink hues—one very pale, one light, and one medium value. Apply a base coat of the light-value pink. To produce the blended effect, randomly brush on the pale and medium values of pink using a 4-inch-wide paintbrush. Working quickly, while the paint is still wet, gently pounce the paint to blend the colors using a homemade pounce tool made from a wool-fabric-wrapped sponge. The flowers can be stamped in either a random pattern or on a measured and marked grid.

4 | Idea Gallery

Customizing a room's decor to make a unique style statement is the goal of every decorating endeavor, and each project presents a different set of challenges. Painted wall treatments offer unique opportunities for self expression and are a creative way to coordinate color schemes, decorating themes, and design motifs. On the following pages you'll find a gallery of clever ideas to kindle your imagination and offer practical solutions for some common decorating dilemmas.

Faux-Window Accent Wall

An oversize stencil creates a focal-point wall that serves a dual purpose in the living room below. It adds large-scale pattern that complements the midscale drapery fabric and small-scale patterns on the accent pillows, and it brings together the overall color scheme. Large-scale stencils applied to entire rooms can sometimes overwhelm the eye, but when used in small areas they can yield high impact without taking over the space.

A multicolor stenciling method is used to produce the effect shown. The largest design areas are first stenciled using a single color. The smaller design elements are then stenciled using two colors applied randomly and blended together to create a variegated effect.

With a little imagination solid-color walls can go from bland to bold without changing the base-coat color. Using cues from the room's color scheme and applying a decorative paint treatment, you can refresh any room in a flash.

Chair Rail

It's as easy as applying an extra coat of paint to add balance and symmetry to single-color walls. Painting the top portion of the wall with a lighter color and dividing it with a chair rail gives the room a new look in no time.

To complete the effect use flat-finish paint for the walls and gloss-finish paint for woodwork. The combination of gloss and matte sheens imparts a refined look that finishes the project in style.

Crinkle

Break up solid-color walls by introducing visual texture and shading. Employ a textural glaze technique, such as rag rolling or sponge painting, and choose a top-coat color that is closely related to the base-coat color for a subtle but intriguing result.

Here a light color paint-and-glaze mixture is applied over a darker base coat. The same color combination applied dark over light would yield a completely different look.

Dot Border

A bold geometric border, painted at chair-rail height, creates a focal point and pops the room's color scheme into focus. The border's palette is picked from the collection of colors in the drapery.

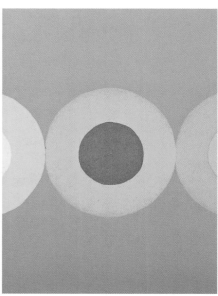

For the initial layout draw a level line at chair-rail height, then mark the circle centers at regular intervals. Use a compass to scribe inner and outer circles at each interval before filling in the designs coloring-book style.

Creatively used black and white design elements offer instant drama to plain walls. Whether ornate and feminine or graphic and modern, borders, stripes, or framed panels painted in black and white make a design statement that is bold and confident.

Paneling Makeover

Wide black and white polka-dot stripes arranged between narrow white pinstripes camouflage the wood paneling on the dining room walls below. The stripes dress up the dated paneling and coordinate with the room's bold black and white color scheme.

After laying out all stripes using a level to ensure that they are plumb and parallel, use painter's tape to tape off the wide stripes. Base-coat the wide stripes with white and allow to dry. Apply office supply stickers at regularly spaced intervals, and then paint the stripes black. When removed the stickers reveal a dot pattern. Handpaint the narrow stripes white.

Filmstrip Wall

The painted filmstrip border in the boy's room below serves a dual purpose. It adds a decorative element and is also a foundation to display wall art. To lay out the design place furniture first, then wrap the filmstrip sections around it. Determine the width of the filmstrips based on the size of the art they will frame, allowing for sprocket-hole borders.

The painting sequence for this design calls for taping off and base-coating the wide strips first. After the base coat is dry, the sprocket holes are measured and marked, then taped off and painted.

Let the textile patterns in your room's decor spark your imagination to go beyond the furnishings and accessories and carry over onto the painted wall treatments. Painting fabric-inspired designs on walls is a great way to tie a color scheme and pattern theme together for a cohesive look.

Freehand Designs

Inspired by the bed linens, the freehand-painted designs in the teen bedroom below extend the pattern mix to the walls. The pastel yellow color scheme of the wall's paint treatment allows the pattern to recede into the background while the room's textiles take center stage.

Although this wall treatment is handpainted, the design starts with a basic measured-and-marked layout. The vertical stripes are plotted on the wall first, then guide marks are made at regular intervals along the edges of each stripe for painting the curly offshoots.

Random Dots

A random pattern of casually painted dots lends an air of whimsy to the girl's room below while echoing the upholstery, accent pillow, and bedding fabric. To prevent the pattern from becoming overwhelming, keep the painting palette light. After painting the dots soften the effect by brushing a top coat on each one using a mixture of white paint and glaze.

Even though the dot pattern is random, the exact placements are first planned using cutout paper circles. When laying out the design, ensure easy repositioning by using removable tape to secure the circles onto the wall. When you are satisfied with the placements, use chalk or a colored pencil to trace the circles before painting.

SCALE: 1 inch = 1 inch   *(from page 132)*

HORIZON LINE

SHORE LINE

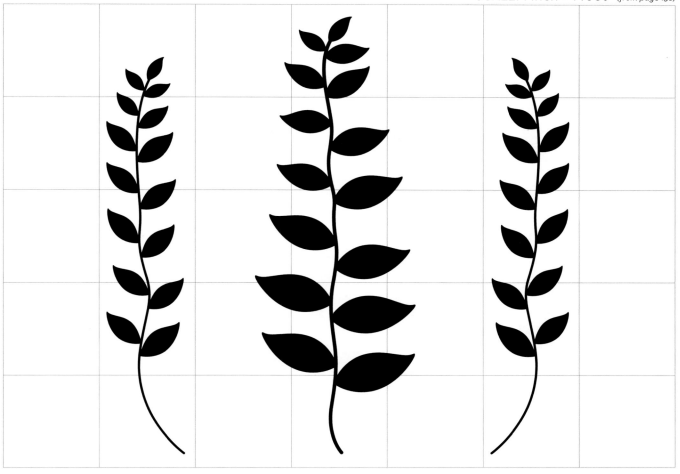

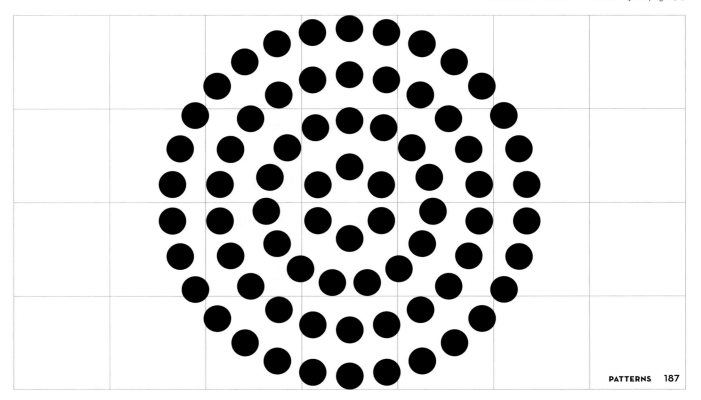

SCALE: ½ inch = 1 inch *(from page 162)*

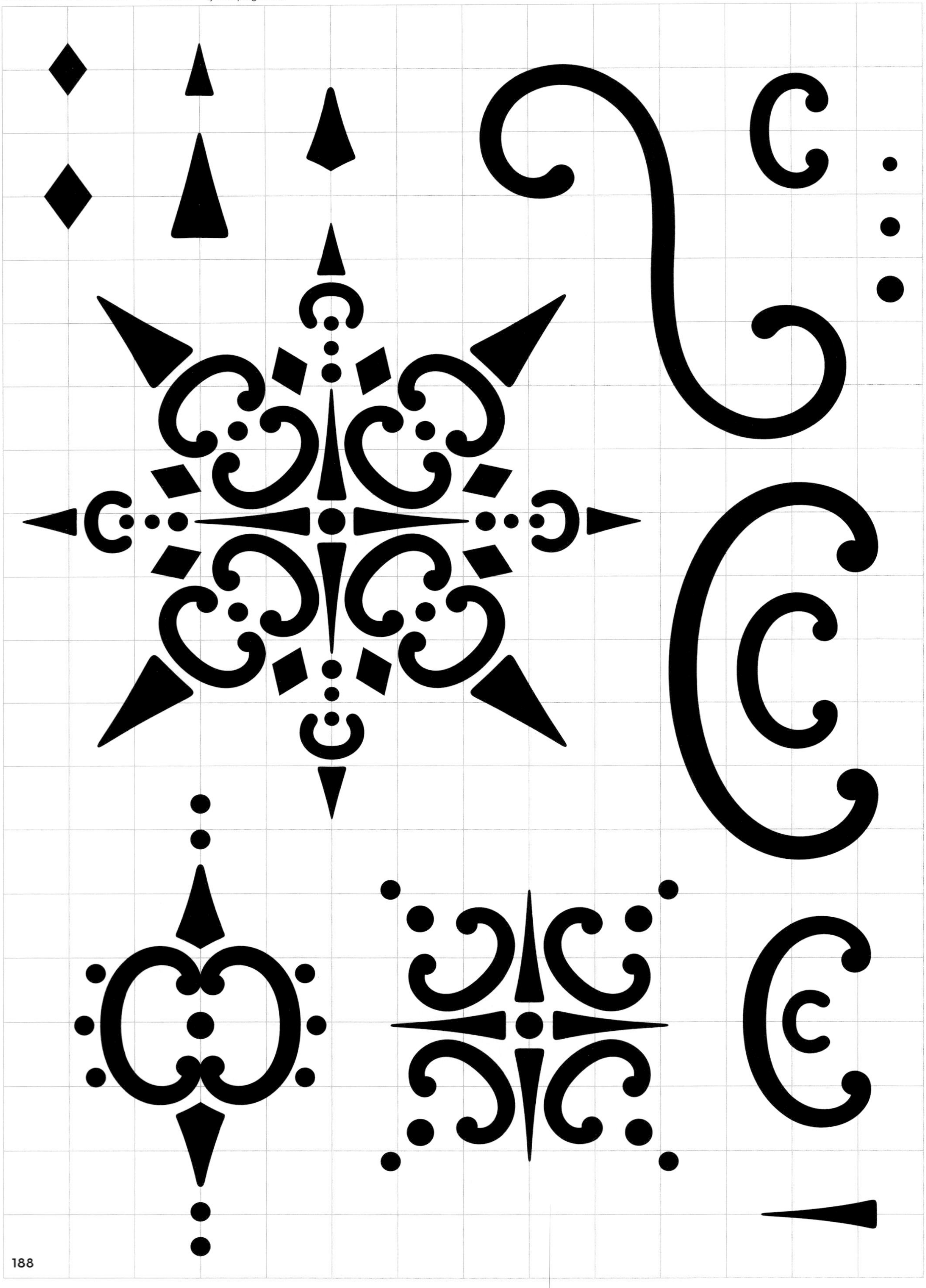

SCALE: ¼ inch = 1 inch *(from page 164)*

6 Resources

Faux Fabrics

Linen
Base Coat: Olympic Brandied Pears #C15-2
Glaze Coat: Olympic Spiced Vinegar #C14-3

Dry-Brush Linen
Base Coat: Sherwin-Williams Gleeful #SW6709
Top Coat: Sherwin-Williams Extra White #SW7006

Denim
Base Coat: Olympic Niagara Falls #A53-2
Glaze Coat: Olympic Serene Sea #B53-3

Suede
Base Coat: Sherwin-Williams Clary Sage #SW6178
Top Coats: Sherwin-Williams Illusions Soft Suede
  Ornamental Kale #7167 & Green Tortoise #7166

Leather
Base Coat: Sherwin-Williams Fame Orange
  #SW6346
Glaze Coat: Sherwin-Williams Renard #SW6348
Glaze Coat: Delta Ceramcoat Acrylic Paints
  Burnt Sienna #02030

Silk Strié
Base Coat: Glidden Light Navaho #731
Glaze Coat: Glidden Cognac Brandy #526

Color Blends

Rag Rolling
Base Coat: Valspar Fragrant Coriander #3002-6A
Glaze Coat: Valspar Butternut Tree #3002-5B

Graduated Color
Base Coat: Olympic Pale Moss Green #C68-2
Top Coat: Olympic Quaking Grass #C68-3
Top Coat: Olympic Guacamole #C68-4
Top Coat: Olympic Moss Point Green #C68-5

Brush & Pounce Blend
Base Coat: Valspar Adrift #4006-5B
Top Coat: Valspar Roadster Blue #4006-6B

Brush Blend
Base Coat: Pittsburgh Yorkshire Pudding #113-4
Top Coat: Pittsburgh Pink Punch #135-4

Wovens & Wood

Grass Cloth
Base Coat: Dutch Boy Yellowtail Dam #C7-3
Glaze Coat: Dutch Boy Burgundy Red #A15-1
Glaze Coat: Dutch Boy Brick Fleck #A12-1
Glaze Coat: Dutch Boy Rose Petal Path #A16-4

Woodgrain Moiré
Base Coat: Dutch Boy Just Enough Yellow #C10-3
Glaze Coat: Dutch Boy Golden Valley #C7-2

Woodgrain Wall Panels
Base Coat: Ace October Orange #B17-6
Border Base Coat: Ace Rockaway Beach #36-6
Border Glaze Coat: Ace Wild, Wild West #D12-7
Minwax Aged Oak Gel Stain

Wicker
Base Coat: Glidden Italian Bronze #599
Glaze Coat: Glidden Almond Petal #810

Set in Stone

Brick
Base Coat: Ace Nevada Tan #D17-4
Glaze Coat: Ace Wicker #D17-5
Glaze Coat: Ace Sierra Madre #D12-3
Glaze Coat: Ace Wild, Wild West #D12-7

Limestone Blocks
Base Coat: Ace Ala Mode #C22-1
Glaze Coat: Ace Summer's Tan #C21-4
Glaze Coat: Ace Wild, Wild West #D12-7

Irregular Stone Blocks
Base Coat: Olympic Crumb Cookie #C20-1
Stone Block Colors: Delta Ceramcoat Acrylic
  Paints in Old Parchment #02092, Antique White
  #02001, Green Sea #02445, Roman Stucco
  #02581, Autumn Brown #02055, Gold Brown
  #02054, and Wedgewood Blue #02069

Marble
Base Coat: Benjamin Moore Woodmont Cream #204
Glaze Coat: Benjamin Moore Oak Ridge #235
Glaze Coat: Benjamin Moore Sabre Gray #1482

All That Shimmers

Copper Verdigris
Base Coat: Modern Masters Antique Copper
  #ME205
Glaze Coat: Modern Masters Mystical Green
  #ME434
Glaze Coat: Delta Ceramcoat Acrylic Paints
  Turquoise #02012

Brushed Stainless Steel
Base Coat: Behr Black Suede #S-H-790
Glaze Coat: Behr Luminoso #743
Glaze Coat: Modern Masters Pewter #ME209

Brushed Gold
Base Coat: Behr Gold Buff #310D-4
Glaze Coat: DecoArt Elegant Finish Metallic Paint
  Glorious Gold #DA071
Glaze Coat: DecoArt Elegant Finish Metallic Paint
  Luminous Gold #DGM02

Copper Blocks
Base Coat: Modern Masters Antique Copper #ME205
Top Coat: Modern Masters Copper #ME195
Top Coat: Modern Masters Copper Penny #ME579

Pearl Wash
Base Coat: Glidden Virtuoso #1510
Glaze Coat: Valspar Shanghai Purple #1555
Medium: Valspar Translucent Glaze Iridescent Pearl

Glaze Techniques

Glaze Wash
Base Coat: Glidden Summer Green #927
Glaze Coat: Glidden Serengeti Plain #915
Glaze Coat: Glidden Devon Green #949

Creative Crinkle
Base Coat: Pittsburgh Honey Butter #118-5
Glaze Coat: Pittsburgh Gingerbread #222-6
Glaze Coat: Pittsburgh Pumpkin Bar #226-7

Pickling
Base Coat: Glidden White Mountain #1543
Glaze Coat: Glidden Blue Phlox #1545

Sponge Paint
Base Coat: Pittsburgh Bran Muffin #217-6
Glaze Coat: Pittsburgh Brick Dust #432-7

Feather Duster
Base Coat: Glidden Farmer's Almanac #555
Glaze Coat: Glidden Papier-Mache #651
Glaze Coat: Glidden Salsa #123

Glazed Wallpaper
Base Coat: Pittsburgh Tailored Linen #181-1
Glaze Coat: Pittsburgh Gold Buff #215-3

Stunning Stripes & Bold Blocks

Hand-Painted Vertical Stripes
Base Coat: Ace Mellow Mood #B39-3
Stripes: Ace Zippidy Doo Dah #B31-3

Taped Vertical Stripes
Base Coat: Behr April Mist #450E-2
Stripes: Behr Marina Isle #480E-3

Taped Horizontal Stripes
Base Coat: Benjamin Moore Navajo White #947
Stripes: Benjamin Moore Alpaca #1074

Block Border
Base Coat: Valspar La Fonda Olive #6006 6-B
Blocks: Valspar La Fonda Antique Red #2002-5-A
  and Oatlands Velvet Night #4001-8-B

Intersecting Blocks
Base Coat: Behr Geranium Leaf #430D-5
Blocks: Behr Corn Husk Green #400D-4, Home
  Song #400C-2, and Asparagus #410D-4

Allover Blocks
Base Coat: Olympic Delicate White #D40-1
Blocks: Olympic Panama Rose #A36-5, Bonfire
  #B33-5, Purplicious #A43-3, Blue Bayou #A56-4,
  Golden Glow #B12-3, Brown Mustard #B14-4,
  Lime Green #B68-4, Flower Pot #A27-4, and
  Purple Passion #A45-3

Stencil & Stamp

Vintage Damask
Base Coat: Benjamin Moore Woven Jacquard #254
Stencil Color: Benjamin Moore Tapestry
  Gold #2153-30
Glaze Coat: Benjamin Moore Weathered Oak
  #1050
Stencil: Large Paisley Pack #IN47, Stencil Library,
  stencil-library.com

Allover Paisley
Base Coat: Sherwin-Williams Aquarium #6767
Stencil Color: Sherwin-Williams Hearts of
  Palm #6415
Stencil: Large Entwined Trellis #PRO900L, Royal
  Design Studio, royaldesignstudio.com or
  800/747-9767

Raised-Texture Stencil
Base Coat: Dutch Boy Yellowtail Dam #C7-3
Glaze Coat: Dutch Boy Thick as Molasses #B16-1
Glaze Coat: Dutch Boy Preppy Green #D9-2
Stencil: Leaves Sculpture Stencil #SSC0104, Stencil
  Ease, stencilease.com

Make Your Own Stencil
Base Coat: Sherwin-Williams Hemp Green #6704
Stencil Colors: Delta Ceramcoat Acrylic Paints
  in White #02505, Pumpkin #02042, Sunbright
  Yellow #02064, Opaque Blue #02508, and
  Napthol Crimson #02408

Geometric Stamp
Base Coat: Benjamin Moore Sour Apple #401
Glaze Coat: Benjamin Moore Perennial #405
Stamped Motif: Delta Ceramcoat Acrylic Paints
  Antique White #02001

Aging Gracefully

Textured Age Wash
Base Coat: Behr Wickerware #360C-2
Glaze Coat: Behr New Brick #S-H-200

Faux Venetian Plaster
Base Coat: Ace Oak Bay #B39-1
Texture Coat: Ace Ocean Falls #B39-2
Texture Coat: Ace Smokey Lake #B39-4
Texture Coat: Ace Candlewax B23-2

Torn-Paper Appliqué
Top Coat: Pittsburgh Earthy Cane #313-4
Minwax Red Oak Gel Stain

Sponged Wash
Base Coat: Benjamin Moore Golden Tan #2150-40
Glaze Coat: Benjamin Moore Navajo White #947
Glaze Coat: Benjamin Moore Mayonnaise #2152-70

Aged Frottage
Base Coat: Olympic Winter Mood #D10-3
Glaze Coat: Olympic Mayan Treasure #B14-5
Glaze Coat: Olympic Fudge #D27-6

Porcelain Crackle
Wall Base Coat: Pittsburgh Earthy Cane #313-4
Panel Base Coat: Pittsburgh Tweed #314-6
Top Coat: Pittsburgh Almond Paste #131-2

Freehand Fun

Simple Mural
Base Coat: Pratt & Lambert Indian Ivory #9-31
Mural Colors: Windsor & Newton Artists' Oil
   Colours Yellow Ochre, Raw Sienna, Burnt Sienna,
   Burnt Umber and Titanium White

Geometrics
Base Coat: Sherwin-Williams Well-Bred Brown #7027
Painted Motif: Delta Ceramcoat Acrylic Paints
   Coastline Blue #02574

Vines & Leaves
Base Coat: Benjamin Moore Navajo White #947
Painted Motif: Delta Ceramcoat Acrylic Paints in
   Light Foliage Green #02537 and Forest Green
   #02010

Strokes & Dots
Base Coat: Behr Marsh Fern #420D-4
Painted Motif: Delta Ceramcoat Acrylic Paints
   White #02505

Freehand Flowers
Base Coat: Benjamin Moore Yours Truly #1317
Painted Motif: Delta Ceramcoat Acrylic Paints Fuchsia
   #02481, Gecko #02347, Bittersweet #02041, &
   Leaf Green #02067

Index

find your style

The elements of your style can be found in great decorating books from Better Homes and Gardens.

ADT1046_1108

Available wherever great books are sold